O Beautiful Mess

by Crystal Ray

O Beautiful Mess by Crystal Ray
ISBN-13: 978-1-07208-498-3

Copyright 2019 @ Ebony Rayford. All rights reserved, including the right to reproduce this book or portions thereof in any form whatsoever.

Illustrations by Amanda S. Andrews, MBA. Founder of The Queen's Guide to Life

Manufactured in the United States of America

To my mom and dad for giving me life and love.

To my grandmothers who imparted wisdom and great strength.

To my amazing boys who have been the most encouraging and supportive of me and giving me a reason to continue in life.

Last and certainly not least, to my God who has always been there with me through it all. Encouraging me and helping me to see that I didn't go through it all because I was worthless, but that I am and always have been a rare diamond whose value is beyond measure!

O Beautiful Mess

Beautiful Mess

Born, born into a mess
A mess with no rest
See my parents unmarried, though unashamed
Still I blamed, this mess
Yet and still I lived, a beauty in poverty
To a body that rejected me, neglected me.
Now poisoned, the toxicity of my emotions
That left me toiling, tossing and turning
Day after day my life brought pain
The pain and shame of my mess
Inward afflictions that brought great stress
The beauty of me, who can really see
The hurt and anger that I tried to flee
Its apart of me, it shaped me
To beauty you see
I am not who I was, I'm not my circumstances
You have your opinions, I chose to keep dancing
Dancing on the opinions of man
My children are legitimate, called to purpose in God to bring something new
To the earth, to the world, to the church, and even me
I'm legitimate too, too bad the church couldn't see!!!
Let them see what they see, let them see just a mess
No longer carrying the opinions of man, last time I checked my God calls me blessed.
Yes little o me
A beautiful mess for all to see.

Introduction

The perception of the human mind never ceases to amaze. Often, we as people can view situations or people at face value or what we heard about them. Completely holding falsehood as truth just because of a what we saw or heard. More often than not, we begin to place borrowed offenses on others, judging them because of the opinions of others and looking into our situation with blurry vision. To sum something or someone up by what we see or hear is to simply say that there is nothing more than what meets the eyes. I am a beautiful woman outwardly, but more importantly my inner beauty supersedes what can be seen on the surface.

"O Beautiful Mess" is a compilation of true events that occurred in my life. The times in which my life was colorless and even dark. I've endured numerous traumatic events that left me feeling as if no beauty remained. That is until I dared to look deeper and from different angles and what I saw was beauty within the mess, a beauty that never faded even when it looked and felt like it was. Instead, I saw the beauty of something greater taking place and it was that beauty that sustained me through it all.

I hope that you enjoy the beauty of the emotions that I faced while enduring some of my life's most challenging moments. I also pray that you will see the beauty that lies within you and know that your beauty is not depicted by the messes of your life, other's opinions of you, nor the negative perspective that you may have of yourself. There is beauty in your mess as well. Be Blessed!

Chapter 1: Anger Within

My old friend, anger; my longest companion. Anger and I go way back several decades and even into my childhood. It's amazing how long we can hold on to that which is familiar and comfortable, even when it's no longer of benefit. Many of us are unaware or unwilling to accept that deep within, the core of our hearts contain a lot of mess, deeply rooted messes that stem from offense and grow into trees with branches and leaves of all that we deal with or don't deal with daily.

I remember as a child, my mom was addicted to crack cocaine. She was in and out of my siblings' and my life. Sadly, mostly out than in. The first five years of my life are times in which she was there. She was a very fun and loving mom, that is until life took a turn.

I remember wondering as a child, why did mom have to be addicted to drugs? Why did everyone else get to keep their mommy but mine always had to leave? These unanswered questions played in my mind during childhood and even in adulthood because she was still not a part of our lives.

My heart ached when she had to leave us. She would begin to behave in irate ways and steal from the house causing her to have to leave. She wouldn't leave for a day or two, or even a week or two; she was gone for years at a time. I remember having rollercoaster emotions about her; I was down when she left and up when she came back. I would light up with so much joy when she returned, hoping that this time was the time she would stay for good and we would be a happy family. Unfortunately, my great expectations would always end in disappointment. She would stay for a few days and leave for five years. By the time I was a teenager, I conditioned my heart to not care about her comings and goings. As a child, I couldn't help but feel what I felt but as a teenager, I was not going to be as emotionally distressed as I used to be. I wouldn't allow myself to feel the disappointment or the hurt.

I would always get in trouble by my dad for moping around the house and not wanting to go out and play. I guess he couldn't handle my sadness because his response was anger. He would yell, "I don't understand why you keep getting sad, she does the same thing every time!"

I reciprocated his anger with my own, and then I was spanked. This was the introduction of teaching me that anger and sorrow were highly frowned upon.

In my teenage years, my anger raged against both of my parents. My dad never once tried to understand how I felt and my mom was more concerned about getting blazed than she was for her family. As a teen, when she decided to pop back up I was not excited and I showed it. I didn't fully understand that she was sick and that she needed help. It wasn't that she didn't love us, she didn't love herself. She was dealing with something in her heart the wrong way or perhaps this was her way of anesthetizing her hidden pain. My anger and lack of caring or understanding the why to her situation didn't help at all. It would cause her to shrink and shorten her stay with us.

"Good riddance," I thought. "We didn't need any more false hopes."

I certainly don't know this experientially, but I've heard that the relationship between mothers and their daughters can get quite interesting, often resulting in arguments and shouting matches. I, on the other hand, can only remember one argument with my mom.

One day I was visiting my grandmother's house, my mom's mom. My family and I were chilling as usual, watching television until we heard the doorbell rang. My cousin answers the door and you know who enters the home very excited to see her family. My family is shocked, but very happy to see her as well, everyone except me. They always made a big deal about it, even calling my older brother so that he could see her. They hugged and embraced her and I simply said, "Hi."

My mother began coming closer to me, demanding a hug and trying to steal one which annoyed me all the more. I walked away into the bedroom where I stayed the remainder of the day until my brother showed up. I loved my oldest brother very much, it was always a pleasure to see him. My mom saw my response to him and got a little sad. Then he loved on her. I walked off once again. While everyone watched television and laughed, reminiscing on the good ol' days, I remained isolated.

After awhile, my mom came into the room to talk to me. My responses were short and I showed no interest in conversing with her. She left the room very sad. I did feel bad about making her feel bad, but I couldn't afford to let her in my heart. Besides, she was going to leave me again in a few days, so I had to remain tough. Suddenly, my brother storms in the room yelling at me. He was pissed at me for making her feel bad.

"Look, I know she hasn't been there for us and she's made some mistakes in life, but she's here right now," he said. "Right now should be your focus. Life is punishing her enough. How would you like it if someone saw your flaws and mistreated you? So, fix your damn attitude 'cause this ain't helping at all."

After listening to him, I felt worse. I didn't want her to get worse or to hurt her. At this moment I had mixed emotions. Once again I was being asked to suck it up, buttercup. Put on a fake face and ignore my feelings for the wellbeing of someone else. Shortly afterwards, I went in the living room with everyone else and they saw to it that the perfect place for me to sit was right next to my mom. I really had to "fake it to make it" because I didn't want to sit there, but I did.

CRYSTAL RAY

My grandma told great stories, as she always did, and I saw that my mom was happy and laughing with her family. I even allowed her to put her arm around me without pulling away. As we watched movies, she fell asleep next to me. She slept for days, as if she hadn't slept well in a really long time.

This time around she even stayed longer than usual. All was well until her urge to get high kicked in and our first argument began. I guess to curve her urge, she needed to listen to music. As she searched for her bag of cd's, she began to accuse me of taking the bag in a very mean way. I didn't even know what the bag looked like.

"I did not take your bag," I said in a firm, yet annoyed voice.

She kept going on about her bag, so my family asked what it looked like? She described the bag and I said, "I definitely didn't take it, it sounds pretty ugly."

My family then began to ask what was inside the bag that she needed so badly? She said her country music was in the bag and she wanted to listen to it.

"I know you got my music," she said. At this point, I'm angry and yet laughing at the same time.

"Look, I do not have your bag or your music, trust me you got the safest music in the house, 'cause don't nobody wanna hear that but you," I said.

My family chuckled at my response and then put the focus on finding her bag. Yes, I was forced to help look for it. We finally found her bag and she used her irritation as an excuse to leave. I'm sure my one and only argument with my mom may be insignificant in comparison to others, but we both were pretty upset. I was all the more upset because in my opinion, she staged it just to find a reason to leave so that she could fix her urge. How dare she accuse me of stealing and country music at that! I grew up in the hood. Nobody in the hood listens to country music! I would get picked on for days if I was caught blasting that in a stereo or singing along with headphones.

In the hood we bumped R&B and Hip Hop, even oldies for the "ol heads," but not country or rock n roll. We watched BET not MTV and definitely NOT CMT! I was angry and hurt because she could have just left. I was nice to her, I let my guard down and she made me out to be a thief. I didn't care to see her again. I had so much anger in my heart towards my mom, but if the truth were told, I loved my mom very much and I never gave up hope of her getting better. I was simply getting tired of hoping because it seemed as though she would never get better. Not too long afterwards, I felt as though I would be tested to see how I would respond when she came around again. What I didn't know is that day would be sooner than later.

One morning during my junior year of school, I was getting off the bus to walk down the street for school. The high school I attended did not have school buses, we had bus passes to ride public transportation to get to and from school. When I was younger, I used to walk with my head down with the occasional look up to check my surroundings. As I was walking towards the school, I remember a few people walking in the opposite direction of me. Suddenly, someone grabbed me from behind and held me tightly. Instantly, I'm ready for war, ready to fight until the finish. Who would dare grab me in broad daylight with others around? The person that was holding me began to weep. I thought what in the world is going on here. Who does that?

I pulled away from the person that was holding me and then the person took off their hoodie. Low and behold, it was my mom. She cried, she was so happy to see me. I was extremely shocked and rather happy to see her as well. At least I knew she was still alive and well. I started tearing up as well because I thought I would never see her again. I told her I was headed to school and she told me that she would meet me in the same spot after school. I was super excited because I wanted to know where she lived. It was a mystery to our family for years. She pointed and explained where she lived, but never gave me a direct address.

I arrived at school wrecked for the remainder of the day, not fully myself. Thousands of thoughts and emotions crossed my mind. For example, had she lived this close for all these years? Literally 15 minutes away in another neighborhood and she couldn't visit us more often? Moreover, she's this close and no one knew it. Emotionally, I was happy, yet sad, confused, and of course, angry.

Finally, school was out. I walked to the place we were supposed to meet. She wasn't there when I arrived, so I waited a little bit. A little bit turned into 15 minutes. At this point I knew I couldn't continue to stand on the corner, especially in an unfamiliar neighborhood. Emotions began to surface and I almost became upset that she lied and dared to leave me waiting by myself on a corner. Instead of anger, I decided to use that energy to find where she lived. I focused my attention on that mission and not my emotions. I prayed that the Lord would help me because He knew exactly where she was. I walked slowly, trying to discern which way to go until suddenly I reached a street. I felt an inward witness that this was the correct street. Next, I prayed for guidance for the correct house. I walked down the street and saw a house next to a vacant lot. I dared to walk up the stairs and I knocked on the door. No one answered. However, I couldn't help but feel that someone was there, so I continued to knock. To my relief, an old man answered the door. I told him that I was looking for my mom and I asked if he knew her by chance.

"What is your momma name?" He said. I told him my mom's name. "You Deb's daughter? You look like her."

"Yes, I am. Do you know where she lives?"

To my relief, he said, "She lives here, let me go wake her up."

OMG, I had never been so happy in my life! I finally knew where she lived. I was so glad I found her because my mind was warring, thinking that this was either the bravest or craziest thing I've done thus far. My mom walks to the door and lets me in. As she apologized for over sleeping, I scoped out the home. It wasn't a grand home, but it wasn't horrible. It was very old and outdated and it smelled as such. I called my family and told them where I was and to my surprise, they did not believe me. So, I handed her the phone to talk to them. I sat and talked with her for a while.

Shortly afterwards, we walked to Taco Bell so that I could eat some dinner. For once in a very long time, we enjoyed each other's company without grudges and without strife. I left very happy. Now that I knew where she was, I could visit her instead of waiting on her to visit me. My sister was so happy. I took her to visit as well, we even stayed the night.

A year later, I was told that my mom was in jail for drug possession. That was the end of my visiting her. She missed out on my whole senior year of high school. While in college, my grandmother sent me a picture of my mother. The back of the picture stated that she loved me and that she was very proud of the woman I've become, just like she always knew I'd be. That blessed my heart and yet saddened it as well. This showed me that she always thought of us even though she wasn't around. I thought that she thought of me horribly, but she didn't. Although I was a mouthy teenager, she always saw something beautiful in me that not even distance or my bad attitude could change.

Since this, I've probably seen my mother only a few times. Three years had passed and she was greatly on my heart. I was away in college and I wasn't around to know what was going on with my family. However, I couldn't help but sense that something was wrong. I kept calling my sister and telling her to check on our mom since we were the only ones who knew where she lived. My sister, being a teenager, didn't get the urgency that I got, nor was it a priority to her. She kept saying she would check on her, but she didn't. I called again a few days later to see if she had done what I asked, again she didn't.

A few weeks later, my grandmother called me to tell me that she had gotten a call from the hospital that my mother was there in a coma and had been for almost two weeks due to her lungs collapsing. Our family knew nothing about it until a very caring nurse saw that no family was around to see my mom.

"I know this woman has to have a family," she thought.

The nurse went the extra mile by calling numbers in my mother's file. Most of them were disconnected. Thank God for my aunt who has had the same number for 30+ years. Until this day, I am grateful for the nurse's diligence. She was right, my mom did have family who loved her dearly. My family went to the hospital immediately and there was my mom, lying lifeless with tubes and machines connected to her to keep her alive. I tried to get to my mom, but I was away at college and 9 months pregnant. The stress of worrying about her caused me to go into early labor. My doctors would not authorize me to travel.

A few days had passed and I got another call from my grandmother stating that my mom's condition was not getting any better and we needed to decide on removing her from life support or not. This was a hard decision. I wanted healing. I wanted a miracle. I wanted my mom to get a chance to live a better life. I wanted her to know my son and the beauty of being a grandmother. In taking me out of the equation and focusing on what's best for her, we decided to give her rest. They removed her from the machines. I heard she fought so hard to stay with us. She was a fighter naturally, but her poor body couldn't accommodate her desire. Her body was worn out and tired.

My family stayed with her for hours until it was super late and people decided to leave the hospital. My mom held on until everyone left and then she left as well. My heart was broken, I was alone, no family and no friends. It was summer and everyone had gone back home. I was taking summer classes so that I could graduate sooner, especially now that I would have a child. My emotions were so out of control that it was hard to stop the contractions. The doctors gave me medicine to slow the labor process. I told them that I was going home to see my family and to attend my mom's funeral whether they released me or not. They understood completely and had me sign documentation and gave me my medical records so that if I went into labor, the doctors would have my history. This was a chance I had to take.

Instead of me traveling publicly, my family drove to get me. This was certainly not something that someone should endure alone. I needed the love and support of my family. A few days after the funeral, I went back to my apartment so that I could finish my last week of summer school. I was heartbroken and enraged by the fact that I was cheated in life. I was upset with God that He had given me a mother that I couldn't see. All of the years I prayed that she would get better, she got worse. I felt guilt, perhaps I should have gotten second opinions, fought harder, believed harder for a miracle or even healing. I was angry because of the way I treated her in the times I had her. I missed out on those precious short moments to just love her for who she was and not for what she was doing. She was my mom and no drug addiction could ever erase or change that.

I thought of how she missed the majority of my life and now she was going to miss out on the life of her first grandson. I thought of how he would never get to know her in person. She would have loved him and all her grandchildren afterwards. I couldn't see past my bleeding heart and the expectations that I had for her that she wasn't measuring up to. I later learned that she didn't have to measure up to my standards or my expectations. Eventually, I had to stop blaming everyone and come to grips that my mom lived the life that she chose to live.

We are all given a choice, no matter how hard it may be. I forgave my mom, but the greatest anger that I denied, was my anger with God. I dared not admit it because who could be mad at God? Who has the right to be mad at the Creator of Heaven and earth and all that's within? I was taught that God can do no wrong and He can't, but in my heart, He did. In my heart, He wronged me greatly. Not only was I angry with Him, I was angry with His people. I was living a good Christian life when my mom passed away. I was going to church, praying, and reading my Word. My church did not send condolences nor did they call to check on me or come by my home. Even my college friends and their parents drove up to help me and they were there for me afterwards. They even helped me after the baby was born as well.

I gave birth to my son two weeks after my mom passed. I started feeling like prayer was a joke because God did not answer my prayers. I poured my heart out to Him, I gave Him my life and yet He didn't answer me. I felt as though He had cheated me out of having a mom. Why did He give me a mother that would miss out on 85% of my life? I didn't ask for her to be my mom. It was only a miracle that I didn't turn away from the church completely and even worse, turn away from the faith. I stopped going to church for a while but I kept my relationship with God. His grace truly brought me through. I couldn't help but see all who were not there for me, while being blinded to the people that were. I learned how to accept what I couldn't change and I moved on the best way I could.

Chapter 2: Boiling Point

I tried to deal with the pain of my mother's death and my new life as a mom the best way I could. I wish I could say that my anger ceased. Although I masked it quite well, the death of my mother caused me to feel an even deeper pain. My mind was in a reverberating cycle. I constantly brooded over previous things in my life that caused me great pain and anger. These thoughts brought me to other things that occurred in my life that I was subconsciously dealing with. The loss of my mom made me think differently about my dad. Although our relationship was repaired, I thought of the days and times that it wasn't.

While visiting my mom after I had found her, she had shared with me that my dad was the reason she became addicted to drugs. She tried drugs with him. The only difference was that she became majorly addicted and he did not. Because she couldn't control her high, he would beat her. I remember watching my parents fight a lot as a child. My dad had a cheating problem and my mom had an addiction problem. I've never seen my dad abuse any of his other women, only my mom and I hated that.

When I became a teenager, I hated him. I became a victim of busted lips. Only difference was that I got beat for liking boys. You would think that I was a fast girl and one that had her way with the guys but I wasn't. As a matter of fact, I was the opposite. I secretly liked them. I remember one day, my cousin and I were walking up the street to go to the corner store. As we were walking, the guy on our street that I liked was sitting on the porch. As we were walking by, he greeted us and we had small talk. I was scared to talk to him, my cousin was doing most of the talking. You know how it is when your crush decides to talk to you; nerves set in.

As we were talking, my dad drove down the street, called me to the car, and told my cousin to go back home. I got in the car and he hit me in the face twice.

"What you doin' talking to him?" he yelled.

I tried to explain that he started talking to us and that we were headed to the store. My dad didn't listen and didn't care. He drove me a few blocks over to my step mom's mother's home. I got out of the car, pissed off and crying. I wanted to hurt my dad. My stepmom saw me crying and saw my face.

"What the hell happened to you?"

She thought I got into a fight with some girls in the neighborhood. I told her that my dad did it and what happened. She was livid. My dad came into the house and she let him have it. I could tell he felt sorry, but he never apologized. From that moment on I hated him. This wasn't the first time

I encountered this, but it was certainly the last thanks to her.

Shortly afterwards, my dad went to jail for other reasons. My family was sad that he went to jail but for some reason, I wasn't. I felt relieved and actually rather happy. I didn't have to deal with him anymore and when he was scheduled to be released, I would be an adult and away in college. While he was in jail, I treated him just like I did my mom. I wanted nothing to do with him. In my mind and heart, I was an orphan.

My dad later turned out to become a man that I grew to love and respect. Thanks be unto God and maturity, I was able to allow him into my adult life. My dad and I are close and we talk every day. I could tell that my dad had some guilt in his heart and so he tried to make it up to us and to some extent I believe he still does. He's always there for us when we need him. My dad had a chance to right his wrongs, unfortunately my mom did not.

I began to ponder the ramifications of not dealing with my emotions. I learned that bad things can happen when we do not manage our emotions and hiding is not management. In my anger, I acted out by fighting and lashing out on people, especially men. I loved and yet hated men. Sometimes you never know what you are capable of doing until it is already done. I was like an angry tea kettle, boiling with the rage of events I had to endure. There was no beauty, just inward rage.

The day came when I reached my boiling point, I was not going to be a victim again. I was not going to be my mother. It was summer, I had just completed my freshman year of college. I went home for the summer as most students did. I stayed a few days at my grandmother's house, my dad's mom. The home in which I ran away from when I was 17 years old. As I stated before, my dad's family was different from my mom's. Unfortunately, his family was filled with drug addicts, alcoholics, drug dealers, etc. Every day, I saw my family fighting and arguing. This was a typical day in the house I grew up in, not to mention it was beyond the legal capacity of residents.

This particular night, I was sitting on the bed in what we called the "middle room." The middle room was a dining room converted into a bedroom/family room. Yes, I once lived in a 2-bedroom home that housed about 20 people. The only privacy I had was in the bathroom. Each room was filled with people. My cousin, who was the same age as me, had a friend over. The guy was like family, he called my grandmother, Granny. My uncle came home in not so great of a mood. It seemed as though he was either high or drunk. He walked through the living room and into the middle room where we were watching television and assumed I had male company over. So he began to be rude to my cousin's friend, telling him it was time for him to go. I told him that he was not my company, that he was a friend of my cousin and that my grandmother gave him permission to stay the night. He walked away, and then came back and told the guy, "I told you to leave."

He began to pick a fight with the guy and me, accusing me of doing things with the guy. This wasn't even my boyfriend. No disrespect to our high school mate, but my boyfriend was FINE and in my opinion, he was not. I ignored my uncle, at some point we even laughed because the things that he said were funny because he was drunk. That is until he started getting in my face, yelling at me. Now I'm angry. I began to walk away because this situation was silly. I planned to leave the house and go over my other grandmother's house which was around the corner.

As I walked away, my uncle got mad and followed me into the kitchen.

"Why are you following me?" I yelled. "I'm leaving."

He proceeded to tell me that I wasn't going anywhere as if I were a child. So now I'm even more upset. My grandmother woke up and asked what was going on. My cousin's friend and I tried to explain it to her.

"I told him that he had to go," my uncle yelled. "Ain't no company staying tonight."

My grandmother began to yell at him, telling him to leave us alone because he was tripping. He didn't like that at all. I started to leave and he hit me, knocking me and the kitchen table over. At this moment, I was livid! I got up pissed, yelling, "Oh, hell no!"

He charged at me again. My family could not contain him, so I grabbed a knife thinking it would scare him. It didn't. He charged after me and I went blank. Next thing I know, blood started coming from his chest and my family started screaming. I didn't realize what I had done and neither did they. In the midst of the noise and chaos, I couldn't hear or think, all I heard was, "Run, get out of here now! Run!"

I ran as fast as I could to my best friend's house. Until that moment, I had never experienced the fight or flight adrenaline. I watched my mother be abused, I watched countless fights from my family going to war with each other. Instead of holding my anger in, this was the moment in which my tea kettle had reached its boiling point. I snapped and this snap almost cost me my life. I don't want to imagine what my uncle would have done to me considering he was under such an influence that several people could not hold him back.

The next day, my grandmother told me that I stabbed him near his heart and that the police were looking for me. I went numb after this event, I thought I was going to jail. My older brother told me that it was best for me to turn myself in and he took me to the police station to do so. He assured me that he was there for me and instructing me on all I needed to do. He also told me to call him with bail information, assuring me that no matter the cost, he would get me out and get me the best lawyer. If you're wondering where my dad was, he was in prison at the time.

My thoughts ran nonstop. I couldn't believe that I was going to jail. The one who broke generational curses and graduated high school and went to college. The one that beat teen pregnancy in our family. The one that always had good grades. While in jail, the realization hit that this was my new future and that all my hopes and dreams had turned in the heat of the moment. My uncle was fighting for his life. The numbness started to melt and I was overcome with anguish. I cried and I cried. I wondered how I ended up there and how was I going to get out of this. How could I make it better? I felt afraid, lost, and alone.

As I cried, I felt the presence of God. I knew He was there, I knew that He was with me. I heard Him say, "Everything will be okay." Hearing those words, I cried even more.

The female officers took good care of me. One of them said to me, "Baby, you don't belong here. You look like a good girl. You have a good spirit."

She put me in a cell alone. There I sat and cried. Finally, after I settled down, I sat against the wall. Not long afterwards, the female officer came to me and told me I was leaving.

"Where am I going now?" I asked.

"You're going home," she replied.

"But how?" I thought. I was so confused. I remembered that I had yet to use my call to call my brother and so I did. My brother was so excited to hear from me! He asked me how much bail was but when I asked the person he stated no bail was needed. I was free to go. No court date or anything. My brother was shocked beyond words. I didn't know what to expect because I had never been in trouble with the law before, not even a ticket. The charges were dropped against me and praise God, my uncle is still alive today and doing well! I learned a valuable lesson about the danger of unmanaged anger.

Some of us have become masters of decorating our mess or masking its existence with good deeds and good services. We often think that because we've covered the debris that the mess will eventually disintegrate and we will live happy and free lives. Don't mean to burst any bubbles, but such things don't disintegrate. They are like seeds planted underground, growing and growing. There is a period of undetected growth and manifested growth. Even though our stuff is covered, it's still growing, growing into something great or something horrible. Contrary to popular belief, even the best of us can only put up a front for so long. What's truly there will be exposed to the light. The beauty isn't in what is exposed, but rather how we respond to what's become exposed. Our response, whether we like it or not, reveals what's in our true hearts.

Life tends to reveal the hidden, it exposes what lies beneath. If you do not believe me, take a good look at your life. Your fruit, how you do daily life, how you relate to yourself and others, reveals the nature of who you truly are and not what you have accustomed yourself to believe. How do you respond when things don't go the way you had hoped? What's your response to the not so pleasant moments? How do you respond to the worst that life can bring? Have you ever had a moment in which you snapped on or went ballistic on someone, only to realize that your reaction was out of line? You end up extending an apology because you didn't mean to be so upset. The truth of the matter is that you didn't mean to show others how upset you really were. You didn't know that anger has been embedded within for such a long time and once it has reached its maximum capacity of pressure, it has to let go. That's the danger of holding in and repressing our emotions.

I've certainly had my days of being pushed over the edge. You will see this as you read my life's story. My only hope is that you acknowledge your own anger or whatever emotion you are struggling with. I give you full permission to look at my life and see how these emotions have affected my life. If you are unwilling to admit that anger may have you hostage, I pray that what's been bottled up on the inside of your subconscious mind will begin to surface, so that you can deal with the mess within and finally start enjoying your life and be the best you possible.

I learned a common misconception about anger is that it's often labeled as a bad emotion and this is completely far from the truth. There is absolutely nothing wrong with being upset or angry. Remember, I called anger my friend. Anger is not our enemy. There are benefits to anger that we will discuss later. If you grew up in the type of home that I was raised in, anger was a confusing emotion because it was labeled as bad, but often defended when reacted upon in a not so pleasant way. As children, we were not allowed to be angry. We were often told to "fix our face." This means to let the anger go and put on a happy face. As you can see, I was taught at an early age to conceal my anger, to pretend it did not exist, and to put on a more appealing or appropriate face.

What our parents, or guardians, didn't know is that they taught us to repress our emotions. They taught us to fake it. Now, as adults we are still suppressing, hiding, and faking how we truly feel on the inside. Many of us are walking hurricanes, active volcanoes, and living tsunamis, wrapped up in the appearance of a delightful, sun-shinny day! Some of us are so good at faking it that there aren't even any cloudy days in our lives. I got five words for that, LIES, LIES, and MORE LIES. What we emotionally hide will often show up in our physical bodies. We're wondering why we can't sleep or eat, or the opposite, why we sleep and eat too much. Soon we have pains in areas and the doctors can't detect anything wrong with us. I've spent so much money on going to the doctor because my emotional deficiency was disrupting my quality of life.

My lack of sleep caused me to over indulge in coffee until I started getting UTIs and kidney infections. The lack of eating due to loss of appetite made me lose a lot of weight. Things got even worse because the caffeine started to eat at the lining of my stomach. I had to go on a bland diet for months to rebuild my stomach lining. Why? All because I was dealing with a lot of mental issues that were manifesting in my decision making. This affected my life all the more.

For a long time, I lived with limited peace and joy. The more I lived this way, the angrier I became, as if I needed more things to be angry about. I got so tired of living this way that I even contemplated taking my own life. Seriously! Who wants to live a life without peace, joy, and all the good stuff? Something was wrong, I just knew it was. I just had a hard time finding the root of it all. I held so many years of situations and circumstances within that I knew it wasn't going to be easy, but it was indeed necessary for me to live a better life. I've come to realize that what was rooted within were previous offenses. Offenses can be anything that has made a breach or violation towards us. Honestly, I had many embedded within, some I've forgotten about or at least I thought I had forgotten about them. You know offense is a sneaky little S.O.B(Son of a Biscuit). Looking back on the moments of my life that brought upon great anger, I realized that they stemmed from what I considered great offenses.

I've always considered myself a very nonchalant, well intact person. I don't get angry, I get over, or so I thought. This was the motto I lived by most of my life. It was a motto I was most proud of. You know, never let them see you sweat, just get over it. By getting over it, I trained my mind to pretend like it never really bothered me or that it never really happened. Now that I am older and more mature, I decided to evaluate the fruit of my method, the method I thought was so genius. I fooled so many people that believed the lie I lived by. Sadly, at some point I fooled myself as well. Now looking back, this was the dumbest strategy I had come up with.

I did not do this intentionally to fix my problems. I did this to anesthetize the deep pain I was feeling within and this was the method that brought about the most relief. I tried to treat the symptoms instead of searching for the true problem and, as we all know, undetected problems often get worse. My emotional pain was an indicator that something was not well, no matter how good my life appeared to be. As true for many of us, we learn to treat the pain or cope with it until the pain becomes so intolerable and then we seek help. I'm here to tell you that this is not okay, people.

Many horrible, damaging things can happen within this process. It's funny how we know this in regard to our physical bodies, but believe it is somehow different with our mental wellbeing. I often thought that it was sad that I learned this because of the hurt I caused myself and others, but the truth is, it is even sadder when we never learn from it. I pray you learn from yours before it is too late. Remember this, the same emotion that caused me to act in rage is also the emotion that helped me press towards the impossible. It's all in how you choose to use it!

Hello Anger, my old friend,
All my heartache and pains has come to end.
You've been with me through it all, so faithful and true.
You pushed me to become who I am, to do what I needed to do.
I thank you for the motivation, you pushed me so far.
So in tuned with you, I know exactly who you are.
I know you're not bad because you helped me so.
But because of the action you've caused, I must let you go.
Dear Anger, my old friend, don't worry about me, I'll be just fine.
Love has lightened the way, it's now my new wine.

Anger, My Old Friend

Chapter 3: Fear or Fight

I can honestly say that fear is by far the most hated feeling. I consider fear the enemy of enemies. This is the emotion that has held me captive for a very long time. After I hurt my uncle and my mom died; fear rapidly intruded. I became afraid of my reactions. I've unknowingly allowed fear to take up illegal residence in my life. Fear is an emotion that does not announce its presence, it likes to disguise itself as something else. Fear is a deceiver. It tricks us in our own voice. It never announces its existence, fear will make you believe that it is your personal thoughts and it's not. So it can remain hidden, it attaches itself to us. Notice the language of fear. Fears says, "I'm afraid of spiders, I don't think things will ever get better." Fear is selfish, it thinks of self. Think about it, if a strange voice in your head tells you audibly that you were afraid of something that would be pretty weird. So the enemy deceives us with our own voice and not the voice of a stranger.

If you are a person who has been through multiple traumatic experiences like me, we tend to have fear-based responses to life. This causes us to make fear-based decisions. No one does this intentionally, it becomes a natural reaction to life. I learned that the number one enabler of fear is denial that fear exists. Not many of us will honestly and boldly admit our fears and yet all of us have them. This is a story I know all too well. I hid my fears. I portrayed how I wanted to see myself and how I wanted others to see me as well. Just like anger, I trained my mind to ignore the fear that I felt and to see it as normal.

"Fear is just a factor of life, no biggie. I'm too strong and busy to deal with fear," I thought.

I'm learning so much on this journey called life. I'm also learning the importance of faith along the way. To combat fear, I wrapped myself up in busyness. Busyness became my new hiding place. I was so busy with my boys, their activities, church, and my job as a teacher. I did this for years. Even though I was growing spiritually, relationally, and mentally, I felt so stuck. I often wondered why my life wasn't going past a certain point. It was as if I hit a ceiling and I couldn't go any further. No matter how hard I tried, access was denied.

I even got super religious with it. I started fasting, praying, and giving more; more of myself and my money, hoping that God would see me and grant me access. I had brief moments of things going well and then came the storms. I went through this cycle for years without fully understanding why it kept happening to me. God has a way of revealing things to us. I was so frustrated with my life, I became angry. I started yelling at God.

"If this is life, no thank you!" I refused to keep living like that.

It was as though He responded, "Well, it's about time. Are you done trying to make it happen yourself?"

My heart shifted. I began to wonder if it was something He wanted to do with me that I refused to accept and obey. Crying out to God in my frustration, I screamed, "What do you want from me, what am I doing wrong?"

I asked the Lord for help and I told the Lord that I wanted to do His will and become who He called me to be. I knew that I was created for more and that what I was doing was so mundane and I was tired of it. Little did I know, He was waiting for me to get sick of myself and my efforts to achieve my purpose. He wanted me to surrender. The storms were sent to me so that I could surrender. I had to surrender what I thought I was created to do, so that I could learn my true purpose. God knew all the pain and anger that was still in my heart and He wanted that, too. God took me up on my offered prayer. I thought great things would happen immediately. Instead, I was kissed with the total opposite. Extreme warfare came. Everything that I had built, the life that I created for myself, came crashing down.

I was served an eviction notice. I was two weeks late on my rent and I had just started a new job. I wasn't due a paycheck for another 3 weeks. Don't you just hate when you start a job in the wrong pay cycle? By this time I was a month late and being charged a daily late fee. I tried to get them to wait but I lived in corporate apartments.

They turned me over to the lawyers on the 16th day. Now I had lawyer fees added on and a court date. When I went to court I was given the option to be on a payment plan until I was caught up. I gave the lawyer $500 upfront and I agreed to have the amount paid in full within a month and a half. The apartment manager agreed to the terms.

We really loved our neighborhood and my boys were in one of the best school districts, plus we were only 12 minutes away from our church and I was 20 minutes away from work. I even worked at my church part time as well. I had to make sure I got the money to keep our home, to fight for our stability. I thought all was well until 3 weeks later when I received a call while I was at work that my things were being thrown outside. I couldn't believe what was happening. I still had 11 days left to pay my past due balance.

I left work with my oldest son, angry and confused. I couldn't believe that they did not call me or contact me at all. They called my emergency contact person. As I was driving home, I kept calling my complex to find out what was going on. They ignored my calls. I called so much that I started getting a busy signal.

When I arrived, I saw all my things thrown on the sidewalk. My neighbors were outside because they threw my stuff out while everyone was watching the solar eclipse. I tried to go inside my home, but they would not let me. The Sheriff was a mean bastard. I asked him where the notice of eviction was that informed me I would be evicted today. I never got one. He yelled at me and said, "Yes you did, it was on your kitchen table when I walked into your home."

I yelled back, telling him there wasn't a paper on my table. The only thing that was on my table was a red bowl of cereal because we were in a hurry and my son didn't have time to finish. I then refuted that with when they entered my home, nothing was packed at all. There were no signs that I was expecting to leave today. He then began to feel ashamed. I demanded that he show me the notice, and then he got really upset. He told me the notice was on the table. I went up the stairs and begged the people clearing the apartment to let me in. I wanted to see the paperwork. They believed me, so they let me in. There wasn't a paper on the table. The table was cleared.

I looked to grab my computer because it had my writings on it. It was gone, I looked outside, it wasn't there either. I tried to remain calm, but by now I was pissed. I called friends and family to help.

The officer approached me and said, "Oh I forgot, I have your valuables in my car."

"Thank God," I thought. *"He has my computer."*

He then approached me with a paper bag.

"What is this?" I asked. "This is not my computer."

"No, its medication," he said. "Legally this can't be thrown out."

My brother and friend arrived and I went to get a moving truck to gather our things. Deep on the inside I was outraged, but I just prayed my way through. My friend and I tried calling more people. We called people from our church but no one helped. Finally, my dad and my sister showed up and we packed what was left of our belongings in the truck. A lot of our things were destroyed. My furniture, pictures, and things that meant a lot to me were destroyed. The only care that was given by those clearing our home was with all my ministry books, cd's, and bibles. I'm grateful because I always dreamed of having my own personal library and I've accumulated almost 300 books so far.

I held it all together, praying and trying to laugh it off, but on the inside I was crushed and my nerves were a wreck. I had never experienced anything like that before; so dishonest, so wicked. In a moment, our lives were turned upside down. For the first time in my life I was not in control. I had to submit to whatever greater plan God had in store. I didn't know what that was or what it required of me. The hardest part was not over because when I picked my younger children up that evening, I had to explain to them that we didn't have our home anymore. I tried to hold it all together, to make it seem like a new adventure. Just as children do, they asked me question upon question. They had questions that I did not have an answer for. As a mother, I felt horrible. I did not have answers nor did I have a plan.

CRYSTAL RAY

We moved in with my sister. Her home was not large enough to accommodate 7 people, but we made it work the best way we could. That night, I stayed in the car. I needed to break away from everyone and honestly, I needed to cry. I sat in my car, angry and confused. I felt so violated, so raped with the public watching. I cried until I fell asleep. Morning came so quickly. I didn't sleep much at all. I then realized that I was now an hour away from work. My short work commute had become a long one. As time went on, I did not sleep much. I had to go through our belongings because things were shoved and mixed together. We didn't know where anything was. I spent months trying to organize and locate our belongings.

This project began to consume my life after work. The more I unpacked, the more damaged items began to surface. I also couldn't sleep because my sister's living style was different from mine. Her family was a lot louder than we were. Anybody that knows me knows that I like a quiet and peaceful home. I do not do noise and chaos. So because the house was noisy with tv's, gadgets, and children, I stayed in the car most of the time. I tried to hold on to my part-time job at the church because I needed the money to get a new home. The boys and I would leave my sister's house at 5:45 am and we wouldn't return until after 9 pm. I was still trying to fix our dilemma by myself until I noticed that my boys were exhausted. I resigned from my part-time job.

I exhausted myself as well and the stress of it all started negatively affecting my digestive system. I was in a lot of pain and I could no longer eat the way I once did. In addition, I knew it was time to leave our church. I got more and more sad and angry with God. I thought He hated us. I spent a lot of time trying to understand what we had done to deserve Him stripping us from everything and everyone we had known and loved. I felt like God had deserted us. I had never felt so abandoned and unloved in all my life. I was greatly depressed, so depressed to where I started going backwards instead of forward. I found myself back in a relationship that I know God removed me from. I was so low and I felt so alone. I needed companionship. I needed somebody to be there to lighten the load that I was carrying. I needed to feel loved.

After a few short months, I came to my senses. I thought because I had started going way left, God would certainly punish me more. One Monday morning, I was told by the principal that I needed to see her after school. All day I worried about what she wanted to talk about. I thought for sure my punishment from God was going to be getting fired. After school, I went to see her as she requested. She told me to sit down.

"Yep," I thought. *"I'm getting fired."*

To my surprise, it wasn't bad news. Someone had paid for my boys' tuition bill for the rest of the school year, saving me thousands of dollars. I was so shocked and beyond grateful for the news. I needed some good news. I had been sitting in darkness for a while and I needed light. The following week, my class and I were talking about prayer, one of the benefits of working at a Christian school. I asked the children if they needed prayer for anything. They stated their prayer requests and a fellow classmate prayed for their friends. After everyone's prayers were prayed, I told the children that we were moving on to our work for the day. One of my students interrupted.

"We didn't pray for you, what is your prayer request?"

All of the children shouted, "We have to pray for you, too!"

That was the sweetest thing ever, it almost brought me to tears. A classroom of 5-year-olds wanting to pray for me. I didn't have faith that God would answer, so I tried to escape their request but they insisted. I told my class that I wanted God to bless my boys and me with a home because we had lost ours. They prayed with their precious hearts that God would help my family. The next week, parents started sending cards to us. They bought us blankets, clothing, and dishes. One particular family wrote me a letter with cash in it and offered to let the boys and I stay in their home that they had listed for sale. They offered to let us stay in their home free of charge until it sold. I couldn't believe it.

The boys and I went to see the home. It was a big, beautiful country home with a pretty nice size pond in the backyard. We were surrounded with nature. I've always wanted a house with a pond or a lake surrounded by lots of trees. The home was beautiful on the inside as well. There was a theatre room in the basement, which became the boys favorite spot. It was so peaceful and the most beautiful thing of all was that we were 5 minutes away from my job. We got to sleep in because we no longer had to wake up at 5am. God had answered my class prayer and the boys and I were so thankful and happy.

Although God had opened the door to give us some relief for our trouble, I was still unhappy deep within. I knew it wouldn't be long until we had to move again. However, I did my best to enjoy the rest. It saved me money for sure. I didn't have to pay rent, utilities, or gas. The boys began to pray that God would bless us with the home. We truly grew to love the house, it felt like home. I didn't have it in me to get my hopes up high only to have them crushed again. The moment we got comfortable in our new life, the house sold and we had to move again. The boys prayed that the people would find another home. I told them that God had blessed their family with that home and they loved it also. ur blessing would come.

We had to go back to my sister's house. My boys were so heart broken and honestly so was I. To make a long story short, our trials didn't end there. However, we did find a great church home with awesome people that love us and we love them as well. Our church became our new joy, they became our family. Things were starting to look hopeful and I was happy again. Then of course more trials came, only this time, I lost my car. My car that I bought brand new and had for four years. A car that was soon to be paid off was deemed a lemon by the courts due to a faulty transmission system. I had already poured thousands of dollars to keep the car maintained, my savings account was depleted, and I could no longer pay for the repairs and my car note. Especially when Ford would not guarantee the longevity of the transmission once it was fixed. I decided to give the car back to the finance company. This made life even harder and messed my credit up even further.

    I had never experienced such a long dry season in all my life. I seriously thought the Lord was trying to kill me. I couldn't see God, or feel Him. I couldn't see my way through. It was as if He had put me in impossible situations on purpose. I had never been more angry with God in all my life. I blamed Him for abandoning us and He was the only one who could fix it, trust I tried and all my attempts ended in failure. Shortly afterwards, friends had become indifferent and now my relationships were up for grabs. Sadly, one of my best friends of 29 years passed away. I felt as though I was one decision away from denouncing myself from the faith. I no longer wanted a God who I thought took pleasure in my pain, a God that was trying to destroy me. We couldn't even get to church because we didn't have a car, we lived far away from church and we could not catch the bus there. I wanted to throw in the towel. I just cried out to the Holy Spirit and He gave me the strength to continue.

I had to see this process through although it was painful, very painful to be exact. I didn't know where I was going, I didn't know anything. I was forced to live day by day. Every time I devoted myself to prayer, fasting, or praise and worship, the fire of my trial got hotter. I told myself to look for the lesson. There is something for me to gain from this experience. I had to humble myself completely and allow the Lord to help me because the fire was becoming unbearable. The moment I set my attention on who was with me in the fire, I started getting a better understanding of what I was supposed to do. As I focused on Him, He began to reveal to me that fear and anger rooted in offenses were holding me back. I finally came to grips with the fact that I had so much built up on the inside of me and that He wanted it dealt with and He wanted it out.

Anger I agreed with but fear I was unsure about. He had to reveal that a bit more to me. Remember my "get over it" methods? You know, out of sight, out of mind? These issues of my life that I thought had died were very much alive within me, robbing and draining me of life and health. Our subconscious mind is our heart, the core of our being. God knew these things were alive in me even though I did not. I've come to discover that God wasn't trying to destroy me, He was exposing what was hidden within. He knew that pain was the key to unlock my heart. I was a hurting little girl wrapped in the flesh of a grown woman. This girl needed to be healed and delivered. He revealed to me that if He hadn't allowed my life to fall apart, I would have continued to live a life that was mediocre to what He had planned and purposed. It would have looked like my life was going great with the nice home, church, job, and family but I would have continued to secretly bleed internally.

If He hadn't brought the storms in my life, I would have never allowed myself to be vulnerable. I never would have fully opened my heart. I was fighting against Him and I didn't even know it. I stopped loving and receiving love because it was easier to not allow people in so that I wouldn't have to deal with the pain of them leaving. I never allowed myself to fully embrace the good times because of fear that the bad ones would soon erase the memories of them. I learned that God knew exactly what to do to break me of myself so that true and lasting healing could take place. It always directed me to Him, I just didn't see it. I learned that humility was not weakness, it was true strength. The bible says in 2 Corinthians 12:9, "His strength is made perfect in our weakness."

He was waiting on me to get tired of my strength so that I could use His. I learned that my answer was not to pray away the pain, or even end it, but to embrace it. Pain was not an enemy, it was a secret ally. What I thought was sent to destroy me was the very thing that brought awareness, healing, and deliverance into my life. So many years of living in fear. It was now time to confront the real issues. Fear had been exposed and so were many others. It was time for me to fight my real enemies. I had so many screwed up perspectives about my life, myself, and God. I was stuck in jobs, places, and relationships that I did not have to stay in.

Maybe you can relate to my story or maybe you have one that is different, yet you have allowed fear to dictate your life as well. I pray that you will begin to make an intentional decision with intentional efforts to reclaim your freedom and the blessings that await you. Remember, avoiding fear is not the correct way to deal with it. Avoiding it will only keep you stagnant, never moving forward. I learned that there is an illusion of going forward that takes place, but in reality, you're going nowhere. The only way to deal with fear is to face it. Please don't waste another day being frozen in cycles of your life, being tormented by fear. Your freedom awaits you, so does joy, peace, clarity of thought, and don't forget, all the love you've ever hoped for. I'm a witness to that!

Fear o fear, oh how I hate thee

Your torment, your pain, the way you raped me.

I remember so clearly the joy that you stole.

Every hurt, every tear that left me unwhole.

But your days are through, your days are gone.

No more fear, thats it, its over were done.

I choose to expose and uproot you too.

For love is my light and my life, my weapon against you.

All that I was afraid of, Ill do it anyway.

So many years Ive wasted listening to your lies every day.

So let love shine, shine bright as bright as the sun.

Forever reminding me of freedom and the victory Ive won.

Chapter 4: Game of Shame

    Shame is a different kind of mess. It's the type of mess that none of us would like to admit. At some point in our lives, we will be met with shame. Some of us are ashamed of our bodies, size, families, failures, I can go on and on. Shame causes us to retreat and hide. We began to hide behind what we feel is shameful. Women are ashamed of facial blemishes, so we'll conceal them with makeup. Shame isn't a manifestation of something outward. Shame comes from inner thoughts, the inward dialogue that we tell ourselves or what others have told us. We only believe in what was said.

    I'm certainly not a stranger to shame. I've lived with shame most of my life, but in denial of course. Denial doesn't justify the fact that something exists. Denial only removes it from our conscious mind while it lives in our subconscious mind. The shame that I denied was alive, well, and operative. I looked up the definition of shame and according to the Merriam Webster Dictionary, shame is a painful emotion caused by a consciousness of guilt, shortcoming, or impropriety. This definition equated shame to some form of misconduct. This definition, however, does not sit well with me. It links shame to an unpleasant behavior, keeping it based upon physical manifestations.

We are all guilty of doing things that are shameful, but my shame did not stem from something that I physically did. It was mental and emotional. To the woman that is ashamed of her body, the body is just a reflection of an inner insecurity. If you were to put another woman, same size, same body shape, but different confidences of self, you would see that it's in the eye of the beholder. Where was the shameful woman's misconduct?

Wikipedia gives a definition of shame that worked much better for me. Their definition states that shame can be described as an unpleasant, self-conscious emotion that involves a negative evaluation of self. I can relate to body shaming. For years, I was ashamed of my looks, my body, and me. I dealt with shame when I compared myself to others' expectations of what beauty is and what's acceptable. I have a small/medium body frame that I call "smedium." When people told me that I was skinny, I would respond by saying, "No, I'm smedium."

I got teased a lot for being skinny. In my eyes, I was not skinny, but everyone I came in contact with said that I was. The only times I wasn't accused of being skinny, was when I was pregnant or during the two years in which I was stressed out and depressed. These are the only times I was called "thick" or "fat." To my big girls, you're not the only ones that get teased about size. That boat really floats both ways. I never understand why big women would shame skinny women because of their own inward shame. I've heard of people being bullied and teased for being overweight. Yes, it's wrong, dead wrong. However, it is also wrong to assume that just because someone's body stature is smaller that they are considered sick or starving themselves. Do those situations occur? Absolutely, they do! Just because it occurs doesn't make it right.

In the white community, being skinny is equivalent to being some type of beauty goddess and is the epitome of all body types. It was the body to strive for, the body that was chosen for magazines, movies, video shoots, fashion, you name it. It's the body that many women compared their own bodies to and that's how the seed of shame was planted. Surprisingly, the black community isn't any different. In the black community, there is nothing cute about being skinny. The foolishness in this notion is that all black women are supposed to be thick and that the thicker a woman is, the higher quality of woman she is.

The craziest thing about this is that thick only applied to women with big butts, big hips, and big legs. If you have big breasts that was just an added bonus. As long as you had those first three, you were considered thick. All emphasis is on having a larger lower frame. Now when there's a woman with a larger upper body, she's not thick, she's fat. I've never heard of this particular woman being considered thick. She's considered badly shaped and unattractive. As for me, I'm a smedium woman with a pretty face and pretty hair. The only true big thing about me is my heart. I definitely know that men aren't looking for that when they meet a woman. You know men aren't looking around saying, "Yea, I'm looking for a woman with the biggest heart."

Most of my life, I have dealt with both men and women, family and friends, teasing me about how skinny I am. Little did they know that every joke they told whispered back to me, "You're not good enough, you're undesirable." What woman or person for that matter doesn't want to be thought of as beautiful? Through the years, I started hating my body. It got so bad that at some point, I started overeating, hoping that I would gain weight in all the right places. That didn't work for me at all. The more I ate, the more my body just metabolized.

When that failed I started wearing layers of clothes, even in the summertime, hoping that it made me look bigger. I even tried wearing bigger clothes to give the illusion that I was bigger and to mask my true size and frame. I got so tired of being teased and made fun of that I started researching plastic surgery. I learned that if you have fat, it can be transferred to more desired areas. I went to the doctor for a consultation, where I learned that the fat tummy I thought I had wasn't fat at all. It was skin because of my small frame stretching during my pregnancies. Not to mention after the babies were born, within a week's time, I was back to my normal size. I wasn't a good candidate for the procedure, I needed more fat. I wanted a body that was considered beautiful in my eyes and others.

Honestly, I am still working on this even now. Of course men, and even women, tell me I'm beautiful, but for some reason it was hard to believe them. I came to realize that my thoughts are messed up in this area. So I am still working on this daily, learning to love myself and accept me just as I am. It's not easy, but it's possible and necessary. Now I can say that I'm a whole lot better than I was. I know that I'm beautiful and I believe it. I now have to trust that someone will love me the way I am.

I developed this insecurity because of previous boyfriends also teasing my smedium frame. Their usual types were thick women. That explains why we went out to eat a lot, ha. Of course they thought I was beautiful and that I had a good heart, but when they teased my size, in my eyes they were just like everyone else. I never truly trusted myself with them. During sex, I would always wear a t-shirt, never fully exposing myself. My beauty was always complimented, but I felt as though I wasn't being taken seriously. I'm closer to 40 years of age, I have 3 children, and I still get accused of being under age because of my youthful appearance. It's crazy! Grown men look, smile, and keep it moving as if I were a child and teenage boys are cheesing big time and flirting. Do you feel my pain? Now when I open my mouth, they apologize and then

I'm a ma'am. My teenage son hates this more than I do!

What helped me realize my beauty was the shade that I received from other women. I would walk around and women would try and bash me.

"She thinks she's cute," they would say.

The hate was so real. I never did anything to them and they didn't like me. I dealt with this the most in high school and in college. Although I was smedium, I could catch guys. It wasn't that hard at all. Lots of men loved my personality, I'm cool, funny, yet chill and goofy. Plus, I know how to have fun. I don't take everything too seriously and I'm not needy. Wait a minute, why do I feel like I'm advertising myself? Trust me, I'm not. Okay, refocusing back to high school. As a teenager, I was small framed but by 8th grade, I finally had breast and they were nice. How do I know? The attention I received from the boys, that's how.

I no longer had to stuff my bra, thank God! I was super happy when they finally came in because all the other girls already had them. Girls with breast were liked, girls without them; not so much. I watched my friends get all the attention, guys buying them stuff. I got tired of buying my own snacks. I wanted to keep my money, too!

"Finally, my time for attention and to be liked has arrived," I thought.

The moment of truth came. I got a boyfriend, too. Not because of my breast though. I did have a guy interested in me before, I just didn't like him then. He grew into a very handsome man that year, too. Besides we were friends, I actually started seeing him as attractive. This was the start of my chocolate fever. By the time we were in high school, my boo was FINE! He knew it, too! The sweet innocent boy that I grew up with who always had a crush on me, was now a ladies man! My family moved almost an hour away and there went our relationship. For a year at least. Life was going great until summer hit. This was the summer that robbed me of my confidence in my new teenage body. In the summer at our new home, many of the teenagers hung out all night long. Every day was just as fun as the previous one.

One day we all agreed to meet up at the pool. It was probably about 12-15 of us teens from our neighborhood. At the time, my female friend and I went everywhere together. We were practically like sisters. She was a beautiful skinny girl as well. We were often referred to as the prettiest girls in the neighborhood. When we got to the pool, the guys were already in the water. My friend walked out in her bikini and of course the guys were smiling. I walked out beside her with a t-shirt covering my bikini. No free shows buddies. I didn't want to draw attention to my body because like I said, I didn't like to be called skinny or to be critiqued.

My friend got into the pool, all the while I'm battling with taking my oversized t-shirt off or keeping it on. Thoughts flooded my mind. It's amazing how the smallest of decisions can cause great stress. I thought about how silly I would look with the t-shirt on in addition to nearly drowning if I jumped into the pool. Everyone wondered why I hadn't gotten in the water yet. I pretended that the water was too cold and that I wasn't ready. Finally, I opted for removing the t-shirt. The minute it was off the boys' eyes were on me and they were excited about my frontal package. They then came over to where we were.

I ignored them. I didn't feel comfortable at all and I learned that I really didn't like the attention. I tried to play it off and be my normal self. My friend, however, had another agenda. She didn't like the attention I got. One guy, we'll call Ethan, came and stayed near me the whole time I was in the pool. Suddenly, she started being indifferent towards me.

"What's wrong with you?" I asked.

"Nothing," she replied.

I already felt uneasy and I didn't care for being around her anymore, so I got out of the pool. All of a sudden, she started whispering something to the guys and they started laughing. I thought nothing of it until they looked at me and started snickering again. One of the girls got out of the pool and sat in the chair next to me. She told me that they were laughing at me because my friend was joking about how big and perky my breast were and that they were going to hit me in the face. I couldn't believe she did that!

Ethan noticed that I now knew what the joke was about. He saw how sad, yet pissed I was. So he came over to talk to me. He apologized for the guys laughing and told me not to sweat it because she was just jealous. He then told me that she liked him, while also admitting that he liked me. I didn't know she liked him nor did I know he liked me. It started making sense, she was jealous. After that, I needed some space from her. I could've blasted out her lack of growth, considering the fact that she was older than I was, but I didn't. I knew what it felt like to feel undesired in comparison to those girls whose bodies were more developed.

Sad to say this was only the beginning to me seeing how she compared herself to me. This didn't stop in high school, it went into adulthood. The only difference was it wasn't about bodies or boys anymore. It was about cars, apartments, pay, etc. My junior year of college, I finally realized how unhealthy the friendship was and I ended it. Although it ended more than a decade ago, I carried the body shame and humiliation for a long time. As an adult, I now see that because of her shame, she inflicted the same on me. Instead of me inflicting people with my shame, I hid it all inside and trained my mind to forget about it. Anybody that came into my life that reminded me of the shame, I withdrew from them.

This plagued me for 17 years. I had so many people fooled that I was a confident woman, comfortable with who I was. I was 33 years old when I finally decided to confront body shame. I did this with the help of the Holy Spirit. I found my beauty in growing closer to Him. This was the beginning of me allowing my repressed issues to come to surface so they could finally be dealt with.

He showed me that I was beautiful inside and out and to not get caught on outer appearance because the heart and character of a person matters most. He revealed the lies that I accepted as truth and commanded me not to view myself in the eyes of society. Neither follow their standards nor compare myself to them. People have the right to set whatever trend and opinion they chose, but I also have a right to reject it.

Beauty cannot be sized up to one image. It's so much more than that and those that do are immature at heart. Think of all the trees, flowers, and nature. All of them are different, yet beautiful. Who looks at the ocean and says, this ocean is shaped better than the others? Beauty was never created to be compared, it was created to be admired, to be praised. God helped me see the beauty that was always there. I just couldn't see it because I was too busy focusing on what I didn't have. Moreover, I learned to give people the right to reject me and my beauty and that my beauty wasn't based upon their opinions. Growing in this confidence, I stopped internalizing everything and I started standing up to what people had to say.

I remember being at my family's BBQ. I pep talked myself into going because I kept distance from my family because of the negativity. I shocked them when my boys and I showed up. Everyone was happy to see us. Everything seemed great, no fights, no arguing, no comparisons. I thought it was definitely too good to be true. I waited for something to go wrong so that I could leave. All was well, until one of my cousins saw me and I'm sure you already know what was said.

"Damn girl, you still skinny."

This was not a compliment, it was a comparison.

This was the moment of truth, the moment of testing. I responded with, "Hey, what's up?"

However, in my mind I was thinking, *"Of course I'm skinny in comparison to you. You're big as hell now."* I didn't say it because that is rude and mean. She definitely would have gotten offended.

The moment of dread came and the comparison game began. I started rallying up my boys because I wasn't going to endure that, but my boys were having fun, playing with their cousins. For their sake, I decided to stay a little longer. Person after person, they made fun of their "shortcomings."

"This is so silly," I thought. *"We're not children anymore, we have them for goodness sake. We are clearly too old for this."*

In the comparison game, no one was called fat even though they really were. They used the beloved term thick. I wasn't the only "skinny cousin" on the porch either, trust me they got teased, too and first. They laughed it off by cussing the other person out. Then it shifted back to a thick person. Back and forth this game went. I knew I was next because there weren't many others left to talk about. Of course I got teased about being skinny, how my butt got smaller, and how I used to at least have boobs, but I guess in their eyes I lost them, too. Rightfully so, I did lose weight but I was secretly battling depression and anxiety and I didn't have much of an appetite. They made a verbal list of what I had and didn't have, once again limiting my beauty to my pretty face.

While they talked and laughed, I had an inner dialogue. Do I really tell them the truth about them and humiliate them or do I just leave and bury everything inside? My heart started weighing on me and what I saw was that they had reduced their beauty to their bodies and at that moment I felt sorry for them. I remained calm and took a deep breath before speaking.

"You know what, I like my size, I like my body, matter of fact I love it, so y'all can kiss whether size butt you think I have or don't have." I turned around, bent over, and said, "Pucker up."

To my surprise, they all laughed it off, screaming, "Girl, you crazy." This was the first time in my life defending my body. This was the beginning of me fighting past negative images and thoughts of myself brought upon by others' opinions. It felt so good, too! I'm not sure what shame you may be feeling or holding inside. The emotions that shame can bring are real. That doesn't mean they are right nor does it make what you're ashamed of true. I've endured more than body shame. I was ashamed of my family for decades. I really wanted to key in on body shame because women are risking and losing their lives to feel desired, to feel beautiful, and most importantly, to be loved.

Don't allow the opinions of others to make you feel less of yourself. When you realize that there is no comparison, it will liberate you in very satisfying ways. Maybe your shame came from sexual abuse as a child or an adult. I've endured both. I was molested as a child and raped as an adult. You don't have to see yourself with abused eyes and an abused mind. You are beautiful because you are you! One thing I've learned to help keep from falling back into this is to keep my mind focused on all the people who love and like me. I took my eyes off of the naysayers. Who cares what they have to say or think? They have a right to be them and you have a right to be you. You also have a right to reject their viewpoints. Return to sender by guarding your heart, not internalizing their opinions, and being the most fabulous you that you can be!

My cry of shame has left me so blue

The lies of my youth that I ate as true

You took me in a room and left me alone

I thought you were my comfort, but you left me to moan.

I hid myself from everyone, thought that would make it better

But loneliness took over making my eyes even wetter.

Your lies may be facts, but your facts are not true.

My truths now come from Gods Word that made me anew.

No more hiding, no more shame, I was created to be a display.

A masterpiece of love to shine every day.

Chapter 5: Ball of Confusion

I know you're probably wondering, why or how does confusion fit? Anger, fear, and shame go hand in hand. I get it, I thought that, too. Until I had to endure a situation that evoked great confusion. If you have, you totally understand what I'm talking about, but if you haven't, keep reading, understanding will come. As you can see, I have quite an interesting life that will get more interesting in this chapter and the next. To be quite honest, one book would be insufficient and would only briefly reveal the multitude of all I've experienced. As you know, life can throw us curve balls, things can change in a moment. I must ask you this. Have you ever gone through something in life that was horrible, yet you couldn't comprehend the reason for it? What I've come to grips with is this, many things will go unanswered and be misunderstood on this side of heaven (or life, whichever you prefer). I believe that this is something that we all must face. Although we may not understand its purpose, it does have a purpose. This is a situation that I had to chuck up as such.

For those of you are chronologically minded, this event took place before the death of my mother and the incident with my uncle. Journey back with me to my crazy college days. As I stated before, I partied a lot in college, typical college behavior. Loud music, sweaty atmosphere, and drunk people everywhere enjoying themselves and having a good time. One night, I went out with my friend, Robin. I was excited about it because my boyfriend and I were on the verge of breaking up. We had a great relationship that I was very proud of and I loved him very much. That greatness changed when he had gotten the news that his ex-girlfriend was pregnant and his parents wanted them to get married. It was what was best for him and the family as a whole, I was told.

His parents wanted the child to grow up in a two-parent home to reap the benefits of that. Because of this, he and I were seeing each other less and less. He graduated and then he moved closer to the city. Our school was in a rural town about 45 minutes away. So as you can see, I was dealing with a lot. I finally found a guy I actually loved and who I thought loved me back. Partying was definitely a way to let my hair down and just have fun, if only for one night. Of course, like us ladies do when we are getting over a man, we make sure we look good and we hang out with our girls. Beyoncé even wrote a song about it called "Freakum Dress" and that was my intention, because "F" him for not wanting to stand up for our relationship and fall into the expectations of others. I was hot and ready to mingle, baby!

Finally, we're at the club, the atmosphere was on point, and the music was banging, not to mention it was a lot on tenderonies on the scene. Robin and I were dancing and having a good time. Two of her male friends were there also. We're dancing with them and drinking free drinks. Don't get it twisted, we didn't dance with them all night. We were not on a boo'ed up mission. These girls just wanted to have fun! We were having fun, at least I was until my "boyfriend" showed up. I say, "boyfriend" because at this point, I didn't know what we were. He sees me dancing with a guy, so he walks up to me and takes me from the guy I was dancing with. Then gives me a hug and a kiss and tells me I look good and how he misses me.

In my mind, I'm thinking, "you jealous little hater," but my response was, "I know." Seeing that I wasn't too happy with what just happened and he already knew how I felt about the other situation, he asked if we could go somewhere and talk. I accepted the offer and we went outside to talk to get away from the noise. He started by apologizing for being distant and for his behavior towards me. Then he stated how confused he was because he really cared about me and loved me a lot, but he never wanted a divided family. I told him that I understood completely but I didn't come out of the house to hear this and that we can talk about it later.

I went back in and started dancing again. He watched me dance with guys all night long. Then came a slow song. He made sure that no one was that close to me as usual. He never minded me dancing with guys on a fast song, but the slow ones he minded very much. I accepted his dance because I truly missed him and we hadn't been close in a few weeks. A few weeks can sometimes feel like forever. When the dance is over and the club was closing, I asked him if he was coming to my place afterwards.

"No, I'm gonna hangout with the bruhs," he said. "I promised them I would come by." I then stood up in his face. While wagging my finger in frustration, I yelled.

"What do you mean, you promised the bruhs? We haven't spent time together either."

Our fight was saved by another fight that broke out on the parking lot.

Robin ran over to me, yelling that we needed to leave. I went out to the parking lot and cops were everywhere. I saw a guy with a bloody t-shirt on, screaming at the top of his lungs. When he turned around I noticed it was the guy I was dancing with earlier, Robin's friend. Robin hurried me in the car and we drove off. Really concerned about the nature of her friends, we drove over to the other guy's apartment, the one who wasn't hurt. When we arrived, to my surprise, the apartment was filled with other drunk, yet concerned people.

We heard the story of what happened. The guy with the bloody shirt was acting extremely crazy, he was still yelling. The fight was clearly over, so I wasn't sure what was wrong with him. I walked over. His eyes were extremely red and he kept yelling, "it burns, it burns!" I immediately told them to flush his eyes out with cool water. It was evident that something was burning his eyes. While trying to flush out his eyes, these drunk fools were borderline drowning the dude. I really felt bad for him.

"What happened to your eyes?" I asked.

"The cops maced me when they tried to clear the crowd and these things in my body are burning, too." he said.

"What's burning in your body?" I thought. *"Pepper spray is usually sprayed not inserted."*

So I went closer to him to try and figure out what he was talking about. He was right, there were metal looking bullet things attached to his skin. Suddenly, the cops showed up due to the noise, alerting everyone that did not live in the apartment that they had to leave immediately. I started talking to the officer about the incident, she was understanding but it was late and the incident caused a disturbance of peace. She still insisted everyone leave. She attempted to get the guy, who I will call Damon, to quiet down but he wouldn't and neither would those who were concerned about him. I knew that this was only going to get worse, so I told the officer that Robin and I would take Damon to my apartment. Hoping that would cause everyone to leave without being forced since he had just declined medical treatment. I thought that was odd, but maybe he didn't have insurance.

Before leaving, the officer said, "We're not gonna get called to your apartment next, are we?"

I assured her that they would not. I didn't know all of those people and they weren't coming over. She laughed at my response and then told everyone that if they were not gone in two minutes they were going to jail.

The officers trusted my judgement. They saw how I helped and I even got Damon to calm down. I didn't even know I had it in me; such assertiveness, such leadership. Robin and I plus the two guys headed over to my place. They were guests in my home before. They came over with Robin a time or two, so I was ok with them visiting. I immediately attended to Damon, trying to figure out what was attached to him and how to get them out. At the time, I was a nursing major, but even if I wasn't, it was still in my nature to help.

Robin, seeing that I had everything under control, took off with the other guy. I finally got those things out of Damon's skin. I then cleaned him and bandaged him up. As I was helping him, he thanked me several times. He even started to tear up.

"I've never had anybody care for me like this before," he said.

"No worries, now you have."

He stated it again, only adding, "How can I repay you?"

I told him that no payment was required and that I was only happy I could help and even more happy that he was feeling better. Next, he shifted the conversation.

"You are so beautiful, I thought you were beautiful from the first day I saw you on campus," he said.

"Thank you for the compliment."

"Please let me repay you," he said.

Trying not to be irritated, although at this point, I was. I said, "Okay dude, you're drunk and in your feelings, shut the "f" up. Let me get you a blanket because I don't think they're coming back. Just rest until daybreak."

He laughed. "Yes, ma'am. I see you got a feisty side, too."

I left him in the bathroom and I went to prepare the couch for him to sleep on. Still wasted, I led him to the couch, turned out the lights, and told him goodnight. I walked in my room and checked my phone to see if my boyfriend had changed his mind. To my surprise, he didn't. I called him to tell him about my crazy night and he didn't respond to my call either. So I got out of those dirty, sweaty clothes. I really wanted to take a shower but didn't want to be naked with Damon in the house. I definitely didn't want to give him any ideas.

I put on my nightgown with the thought of showering first thing in the morning. I turned my light out and I started walking towards my bed. Then all of a sudden, it felt like someone was in the room with me. I don't sleep with my bedroom door closed. Plus, I lived alone.

I got up and said, "Damon, why are you in my room and damn don't you knock? Do you need something?"

"Yes," he responded.

"Ok, what is it that you need now?" I asked.

"You," he said, confidently. He immediately started kissing me. I was thrown back by his actions.

"Dude, what are you doing?" I asked. "You're drunk and tripping! Get out and go to sleep, you need to rest and I'm tired, too."

Then he whispered, "I'm going to make sure you sleep good."

I started laughing in disbelief that number one, he just said that, and two at the fact that this is even happening.

"Did you forget, I have a boyfriend? Who might show up at any minute? He is good for that." Damon then picked me up and threw me on my bed. "No, no I'm not like this, you gotta leave." I said while fighting to get up. For some reason, my fight became a turn on for him.

"You know you want this. I love you."

"I don't want it!" I screamed, "Let me go now!" Now I'm pissed, afraid, and confused. I couldn't believe this was happening to me. I'm not a victim or a piece of meat. I fought even harder.

This guy was a wrestler for the school. I found myself unable to escape his hold and I was raped. I saw that the more I fought, the more pain I was in. I was in a really awkward position and I began crying. To make matters worse, I had this guy on top of me saying, "I love you. Just let me make you feel good. It's my turn to take care of you. I've always liked you, I had dreams that you were my wife." All while I'm yelling, "NO!"

I wore myself out trying to fight. Feeling hopeless, I gave up the fight and just laid there, hoping for it all to end and crying all the more. This guy was beyond drunk, he was nuts! He thought all the stuff he said was supposed to make it better. My tears began to wear on him. He told me that if I just relaxed, I would be happy and not in tears. I tried not to go ballistic because the last time I went ballistic on a man, I stabbed him in the chest. I was in so much fear of the worst happening. To my avail, he could no longer handle my crying. He got off of me, in total realization that he raped me.

"Oh my God! I just raped you." he said.

I ran into my bathroom and I locked the door. I dropped to the floor crying even louder, in total disbelief of what just happened to me. Why did this happen to me? Regret for helping him started to surface. Thoughts upon thoughts, emotion upon emotion raged on the inside. I started praying to God, asking what I did to deserve this. The more I prayed, the more I cried.

Then suddenly, I heard a voice say, "Shh, get out of the bathroom."

I thought I was going crazy, so I ignored the voice. This time I heard, "Shh, get out the bathroom now."

Very hesitant to obey the voice I heard, I opened the bathroom door and walked out. I had a bad feeling in my stomach.

Next, I heard, "Go into the kitchen." I slowly went into the kitchen turned on the light and to my surprise, there was Damon about to take his life. He looked at me.

"I'm so sorry for raping you," he said. "I did not mean to hurt you. You were good to me. I can't believe I did this to you, I'm so sorry. I don't deserve to live, I'm a horrible person."

"No, please put the weapon down, I forgive you," I said. "Please don't kill yourself."

My kindness made him burst into tears. "After what I did to you, you're still being nice? Why are you being nice?"

I talked to him about forgiveness and Jesus. Shortly afterwards, he put the weapon down and started weeping a lot. As he was weeping with his face in his hands, I ran and picked up the weapon.

"I'm going to jail," he said. "I won't finish school and I won't be able to play sports again."

I gave him my word that I would not press charges on him and he left, totally confused at the fact that I remained kind even after it all.

I locked the door behind him, ran into the bathroom, turned on the shower, and cried and cried. I stayed home for several days in total isolation from others. I didn't go to class and I didn't talk to my friends. Finally, I told my two best friends what happened to me and I went to class. I told my professors that I suffered the tragedy of rape and they were very understanding and accommodating, only to experience unwanted sexual contact again with a female professor. I'm sure she really felt sorry for me, but her hugging me in her office with her pelvis pressed into mines added insult to injury.

My best friends, however, knew the details of the entire event. I didn't share this with anyone else because I did not understand it, plus I was ashamed. I didn't understand why God allowed this to happen. I shocked myself, why didn't I injure or kill him? Why didn't I react in anger like the many other times people hurt me? I had no desire to hurt him, not one. One thing is for certain, I finally learned that vengeance was not mine, it's the Lord's. I kept my word, I did not talk to the police.

A few days later, I heard that he had left school and went back home to California. In a short time I was able to walk out the forgiveness that I talked to him about. What I couldn't see at the time was that he did not need to die in my home. That would've been no good for me, considering that I already had a record for stabbing a man. It would have been as though I snapped because he raped me and killed him. His life would have been gone and so would mine. We both got the opportunity to live the lives that we were created to live. You know being raped violates not only a woman's body but every aspect of her being. This violation is beyond words. I can't even begin to express what this feels like. It takes away that woman's virtue and value, leaving her to feel lower than low.

Honestly, after this I never fully trusted men, not even my "boyfriend" who showed up the following weekend, unannounced and uninvited. He knocked on the door, thinking I would be happy to see him. I pretended I wasn't home. Then I thought about it. He's going to call my cell phone and my ringer is on. That's exactly what he did. He knocked again.

"Babe, I know you're in there, please open the door," he said. I opened the door and he said, "Dang, can a "n" come in?"

I let him in and I walked to my room and got in the bed. No hug, no kiss, no nothing. He noticed that I wasn't being myself. He thought it was because I was still mad at him for not coming home with me or talking to me since that night.

"Damn, I can't even get a hello?" he asked. He sat on my bed, asking me what my problem was. I snapped and started yelling and hitting him. "What the hell is wrong with you?"

"You weren't there for me, you didn't protect me, it's your fault I got raped," I let slip. "If you would have come home with me, none of this would've happened!"

As you can see, I may have forgiven Damon, but I blamed it all on my boyfriend.

He got quiet and then he yelled, "What? Babe, who raped you?"

I burst into tears afterwards. He tried to keep his cool, but I could tell he was confused and outraged. His voice started to weaken as if he wanted to cry but held it in.

He asked me in an angry voice, "Babe, please to me what happened? Who raped you?"

"Just hold me," I responded.

He held me tight and in a weak voice, he said, "Please tell me. I gotta fix this, I can't fix it until you tell me."

I mustered up enough strength to tell him. Boy was he pissed!! I made him promise that he wasn't going to do anything stupid and told him that the guy ran away to California. I gave the forgiveness talk to him as well, except he wasn't having it. By the look in his eyes, I really hoped the rumor was true of the guy moving back to Cali.

He kissed me and said, "I'll be back in a little bit."

I begged him to stay with me. He laid there with me, holding me until I went to sleep. When I woke up later that evening, he was gone. He didn't answer his phone either. I knew him, he needed some space to process all that I revealed to him.

A few days later he called me, apologized, and said that he needed to process and also that he found the guy. I knew he was from California but never would I have imagined that he would find that guy. I'm pretty sure that Damon was shocked as well. I asked him what did he do? He assured me that he did nothing but his homeboys in California found Damon at his request and beat him up. I was afraid they killed him but he promised me the guy was still alive. All I can say is thank God his life was spared once more and I pray this guy chose the right path in life.

    I don't know why I had to experience that. The confusion was driving me crazy. I didn't understand why I got raped but mercy was extended greatly to Damon. Honestly, I had to let it go and stop thinking about it. Although I chose to let it go, this experience shaped and changed my life completely, especially my view points on men. This ignited a season in my life of pure wildin' out. I no longer cared what men thought or how they felt. I used them as I was used. The only difference is that I threw them away after I was done. The good girl went bad! Men become pure fun and entertainment to me. I had no time for love, just fun, until God came and revealed His plan to me for marriage and that I was to save myself for the man He had for me.

Chapter 6: The Sweetest Romance

My bad girl days were short lived. I can thank my first and second pregnancies for that. After years of isolation and trying to be the best mother I could be to my two boys, I dared to love again. A year had passed since I left, what was then, my youngest son's father. To sum that relationship up, I fell for a man that wasn't for me it all. My son is the beautiful fruit that remains from that lesson learned. I moved back to my college town in hopes to finish school and start a new life. The stress and strain of that relationship drained me completely. I needed and wanted something new. After moving back, I had a really hard time finding employment, I was extremely behind on my car note. I was so afraid of getting my car repossessed. My son's father and I were not on good terms. I now was a mom of a one-year-old and a three-year-old. I was 24 years old with two young children. I was away from family and friends, but I knew I was in the right place.

At first the move was really hard, it was new. I still had a lot of learning to do plus mother two children. The stress of my life caused me to have migraines. Migraines are horrible. I realized that I had drifted away from the Lord and that I needed Him desperately. I kept feeling as though I needed to go to church. I didn't know what to expect, but I knew that it would help. I needed to get back on track. I prayed to God on a Saturday night that I really wanted to go to church. The church that I attended in college with old friends was an hour away. I only had $5 to my name and that certainly wasn't enough money for gas to drive 2 hours. I went to bed that night with the expectation of something great happening. I woke early Sunday morning with my heart set on going to church. I knew I didn't have enough money for gas, so I prayed to God that He would supernaturally get us there and back home.

I got us ready for church and I drove to the gas station. I walked up to the window and I asked for $5 on pump 3. The guy said okay and handed me a $5-dollar bill in change.

"Sir, why are you giving me my $5 back?" I asked. "I need it for gas."

"Ma'am, that's your change, you handed me $10."

Confused as can be I asked, "I did?"

"Yes," he replied. "Have a good day."

I then gave him the other $5 to get more gas. I thought I was losing my mind. I know I only had $5 to my name. I walked to the car to pump the gas. While the gas was pumping, I started searching my purse and the car for the $5-dollar bill I knew I had. The gas pump was finished so I decided to forget about searching for the $5. The whole car ride I was seriously shocked, but very grateful. I knew we would make it to church and back home. With supernatural intervention, I knew God had intended for me to be there. We arrived and I was so happy. I was greeted by those who knew me previously. They were shocked that I had another baby. Some greeted us while others talked about the fact that I came back with another baby.

Service started and it seemed to be a special occasion. The worship was great. There was a man in an army uniform jumping around and praising God. The pastor announced that his son was finally home from the military. Everyone cheered, some even started praising with him. I didn't know their son, because I never met him. I had been gone from the church for quite some time. When I looked at him, I was shocked. It was the guy that was in my dreams two years prior. I had a series of dreams about this man before I even knew him. I had dreams that we were in a relationship and that we had a son together. This was a freaky Sunday! Being in the presence of God, my headaches stopped as well. This was an amazing Sunday!

After service, I drove back home, trying to understand it all. I was a super babe in the faith and I experienced things that I could not comprehend. All week long, I pondered upon the weirdness of it all. I was so grateful for God helping and healing me. I began to attend church faithfully. I was growing so much in the Word and my relationship with Him. Doors that were once closed and delayed started opening.

O BEAUTIFUL MESS

I got a new job as a teacher. It came with a huge commute, 2 ½ hour daily commute to be exact, but I was thankful for employment. I drove that commute faithfully for six long months; three seasons, fall, winter, and spring. In April, I got approved for an apartment in the town where I worked, also making me closer to my beloved church. Life was great! Now that I was closer to church, I started volunteering. I loved helping others. While I was a kid, I loved singing in the choir, so I decided to join the choir. My first choir rehearsal, I met some really cool people. I'm a soprano so they showed me where to sit. Everyone was friendly. I sat on the second row next to a girl I already knew. Rehearsal was about to start, and then all of a sudden, the army guy walks in hugging and high-fiving people. He then sat right behind me.

Why did he sit right behind me? My nerves were in an uproar and I dared not look back. I couldn't believe how I was behaving. I acted like a scared school girl, trying my best not to draw attention to myself. After rehearsal, everyone talked a bit and said their goodbyes. That's when he looked at me. For the first time, we were eye to eye. I was so afraid, I looked away quickly. My heart was pounding. While walking away, I dared to look his way again, and then he cut the cutest smile, I smiled back.

Several choir rehearsals later, I had to bring my boys along, too. My oldest son sat in the pews and my youngest son sat with me. Of course, everyone played with the baby. Then the guy wanted to play with him. After this, I was less afraid to talk to him. I tried my best to hide from him and to avoid conversations. However, every time he saw my boys, he would always compliment their haircuts and their shoes. This made it even harder to avoid him because my boys loved playing with him.

Fast forward to summer, as a matter of fact, my favorite holiday, Independence Day. The church had allowed us to pop fireworks on the parking lot. We could also watch the fireworks show from the parking lot as well. The boys and I had a blast. Moments later, the pastor's sons pulled up and began to greet the people. My boys were excited to play with their new buddy. I asked my friend to walk across the street with me to get the boys some food. The boys stayed on the parking lot with the other kids and continued to play.

"You ok?" my friend asked.

"Why?" I asked. "Do I not look okay?"

She replied that I was acting a little quiet. So I explained to her the dreams I had almost 3 years ago. I revealed that the guy, we'll call Derrick, was in those dreams and I didn't know him then. I explained everything to the freaky Sunday and how I can't run from this guy even if I tried. She was so amazed, yet so excited about all that I shared with her, letting me know that none of this was a coincidence. I didn't really believe in coincidences nor did I believe in fate.

Walking back to the parking lot, I uttered, "I think this may be my husband."

She really started screaming in joy because it made such sense. By this time, it was starting to get dark and everyone awaited the fireworks show. I watched the fireworks with my boys, my friend, and her kids. That's my favorite part of the holiday. I watched the fireworks, yet I was afraid of the conclusion that my friend and I came to. I couldn't believe that God would put me, a girl from the hood who dated hood guys, with not only a church boy, but a church family. The more I thought of it, I felt like I didn't measure up. I was in my mid-20's at the time. I did not have the confidence that I later developed. In my mind, I thought that this guy and his family were too good for me.

After the fireworks show ended, everyone started cleaning up their messes, preparing to leave. Some other young adults approached my friend and I and asked if we wanted to go bowling with them. We agreed to go. Derrick walked over to where we were. I wasn't familiar with the city at all because I was still new. They tried to explain to me where the bowling alley was. However, Derrick gave me his number and told me to call him if I got lost, and then he said goodbye to my boys. My friend and I got in the car and started screaming together. I couldn't believe he gave me his number. I never flirted with the guy or showed any interest. I convinced myself that he was just being nice and making sure we got there.

We drove to her house so her sister could watch the kids and we headed to the bowling alley. I texted Derrick and asked him how to get there. This was before phone GPS systems. We arrived at the bowling alley, so I texted him and told him we made it. He said that everyone was leaving, it was a whack night. We all talked and laughed on the parking lot for a bit. This was the beginning of us talking all the time. He texted me the next day. We texted for a few days and then we started talking on the phone for a few weeks. He was a funny and really cool guy. I could tell that he really liked me. He did most of the calling. We talked and texted each other all day, every day for a month. I was in unbelief that all this was happening.

One weekend, I planned to take the boys to the children's farm. They loved that place. He called me as we were getting ready to leave, asked if he could join us, and that he would bring his nieces, too. We arrived at the children's farm and shortly afterwards they arrived as well. They found us and we walked around together looking at animals. His nieces were too cute and one of them was really funny and sassy. The oldest niece called my name and said, "I have something for you." She reached in her pocket and handed me a folded piece of paper. I opened the paper and I saw the most beautiful crooked heart with these words written in it: "Derrick loves Crystal."

I smiled, gave her a hug, and I thanked her. It was really the sweetest thing. He stood there and smiled as well. While walking, we came near a playground and instantly I paused. He asked me if I was okay.

"Yes," I said. "I just had déjà vu." I saw us walking with the kids and we had on the same clothes as the vision. I started freaking out.

"Let's stop at the park and let the kids play and we can talk." He grabbed my hand. "This was meant to be."

We sat down while the kids were playing. I was so scared of letting the boys loose. I was always right next to them as they played. He assured me that the boys were fine and that I needed to allow them to be boys. We talked with his arm wrapped around me. I seriously couldn't believe this was happening. The kids were exhausted, so we decided it was a good time to leave, but neither of us wanted to leave each other. It was something about him that was comforting and safe. We put the kids in the car and we talked on the parking lot for a while. The kids started to get restless, so he asked me for a hug. He gave me the best hug ever. He had the kind of hug that makes you want to melt. The hug became a hold. He held me in his arms close and I rested my head on his shoulder.

"I feel like I have to protect you," he said.

I didn't know what that meant. No man had ever said that to me before, as has yet to say that to me since. I do know this; for the first time in life I felt wanted. I felt desired.

Later that night, he told me that the girls really liked me and that they all had a good time with us. He also shared his feelings about me. This was the beginning of the sweetest romance. From that moment on we were inseparable. I loved the love that he gave and he loved the love I gave as well. We encouraged each other. Every time I entered his presence, his countenance would light up and he always complimented my beauty and my style. That summer was the best summer of my entire life, I had never been so happy in my life. I thanked God constantly for sending him my way. I had a job I loved, great children, a great church, and a great man. He took me all over the city, summer nights were the best driving and listening to music, hopping out of the car to dance and just being silly. He brought out the fun side of me that I lost. I had forgotten what it was like to just be me. Not someone's mother or teacher. With him I could be me and it was okay. I could tell he felt the same way. He would come alive around me.

The chemistry between the two of us was so magnetic, not long afterwards we became sexually intimate. I tried to hide my body from him, but he wouldn't let me. The t-shirt wasn't working for him. I felt his love and his passion for me, not just my body. I was more than a pretty face to him. He wasn't after pleasing himself like my previous relationships. That man loved me, really loved me, and I loved him too, so much. For the first time in my life, I gave not only my body but my whole heart to him and I knew I had his, too.

At the end of summer, before the beginning of the school year, I realized that I wasn't feeling too good. My best friend told me that I needed to take a pregnancy test. I didn't even want to think about being pregnant. I told her I would get some rest and take care of myself. A week had passed and I still wasn't feeling good. I took her advice and took a pregnancy test and indeed I was pregnant. Sorrow and fear gripped my heart so strongly. I remember the reactions of my sons' fathers when I told them I was pregnant. It was not good and they begged me to get an abortion. Although Derrick and I had been together for a few months, there was still so much we didn't know about each other. I didn't know how to tell him but I knew I had to.

We met up at what was our spot and I told him I was pregnant. He was speechless and in shock. It was the reaction I expected. Then he freaked out. He even threw up. Now that was a first for me. He told me that this would ruin everything. He told me that his family wouldn't approve of our relationship because I was already a single mom but he had a plan for that. Now with me being pregnant, they would be outraged. I didn't fit the family's vision and I didn't fit the kind of woman they wanted him to be with. They wanted their sons to be with pastor's daughters and I was far from one of them. This angered me greatly.

"Am I not a good person, with a bright future?" I asked. "So what I have children, so what I didn't come from a church family. I'm saved. It's not like my family are atheists or some other religion, they believe in Christ, too."

Sadly, I knew that didn't matter to his family. He begged me to get an abortion because of the shame it would cause his family. He would later go to his family and fight for us to be together, but the baby wasn't a good thing at the time. I got so mad.

"Why did you even bother to be with me in the first place if I was considered vermin to your family?" I yelled.

He started pouring his heart out saying that I was different. I was kind and he was attracted to kindness, plus he watched me with my boys at church and he loved how I cared for them. Overwhelmed with emotion, I got out of his car and got into my own, I was crushed. I drove to my apartment and he followed me to make sure that I was okay. I rejected all of his advances to be affectionate, or even intimate with me. Still he persisted hoping that he would get me to give in. I was disgusted by him. I could hear the breakdown of *Envogue's* song so clearly in my head. "Never gonna get it, never gonna get it, never gonna get it, never gonna get it." I laughed out loud as the song played in my head. My laugh obviously upset him because that was his que to give up, and he left abruptly! I didn't care. That was my silent way of telling him to kick rocks. I didn't want to see him ever again.

We didn't contact each other for the next few days. Then he called and apologized, saying he wanted to see me. He told me that I was worth the risk and that he was going to tell his dad soon. He had to do it in a clever way because his dad did not handle his brother's situation to well. The moment of truth came two weeks later. Derrick took his dad and uncle to a restaurant and told them. His dad was very upset. He told Derrick that he needed to leave the church. Derrick told me that his dad would react pretty badly, but I never thought that it would result to this. He lived in one of his dad's townhomes with his brother and he had to leave the home, too. He decided it was best for him to leave town period. He left me pregnant and moved to another state.

We talked over the phone. I'd never seen him more hurt than by this situation. He always wanted to please and be approved of by his father. He would tell me, as a child he could never do anything right. I would comfort him and love him through those memories. We missed each other a lot. He wanted me to move to where he was but I had just moved. I tried to get him to live with me but he said that it was too painful to be in the same city with his family and not be able to see them, even his brothers were upset. I understood. I didn't want to imagine the pain of feeling banished and disowned.

A few weeks had passed and it was time for my first doctor's appointment. They made me take a pregnancy test to confirm that I was indeed pregnant. The test came back positive. The doctor entered the room with a congratulations basket of goodies. Next, she asked me the usual series of questions. The doctor detected that I was in my second trimester. She wanted to listen to the baby's heartbeat. She then told me that I was going to see the ultrasound tech to get an ultrasound. Since I had been pregnant twice before, I thought it was rather soon for an ultrasound. I secretly started to worry.

After getting the ultrasound, the tech told me that the doctor would talk to me. By this time, I was super worried and scared. I asked if I could go to the bathroom first. I went into the bathroom and prayed. I got no relief from prayer, so I knew something was wrong with the baby. I left the restroom and went into the room to wait for the doctor. The doctor's face was not a happy one. I looked at her and I asked if the baby was okay.

"No, the baby isn't okay." she said. "They could not detect a heartbeat from the baby, that's why I ordered the ultrasound to be for certain." She then said, "I'm so sorry the baby is no longer living."

The doctor explained to me that I could have surgery to remove the baby or I could allow my body to abort the baby via miscarriage. She advised me to get the surgery because the other option was bloody and very painful. Confused and shocked by the news, I was speechless. She gave me a hug and her condolences again and told me that her nurse would call me to set up an appointment for the surgery if I wanted. I walked out of the exam room, leaving the congratulations basket behind. I walked to the parking lot, got into my car, and I screamed, crying uncontrollably. I called Derrick for comfort, but he was speechless and it wasn't a good time for him to talk. So I called my grandmother who tried her best to comfort me.

O BEAUTIFUL MESS

A few days before my appointment, I had a dream that my boyfriend died and that we were at his funeral. I woke up praying and rebuking death. I then realized that was probably the day the baby died. The dream was trying to prepare my heart for it. My friend kept my kids for a few days to help me process everything and grieve. She was very helpful and supportive because she'd had a miscarriage as well. The first few days, I just laid on the couch and cried. I didn't want to talk to anybody. By day three, the nurse called to schedule the surgery for a few days away. I finally talked to Derrick and told him about the surgery. He told me that he would be there for sure because he was coming to town for a visit.

The day before the surgery, I didn't hear from him. My friend from church told me not to count on him and that she would work a half day to help me. I had to be at the hospital early, so she came and picked me up and stayed with me. She prayed with me before the surgery and told me that she would be there when it was over. The nurses took me back to prep me for surgery and explained the procedure to me. Derrick still wasn't there. I was alone. As I'm listening to the nurse and following her instructions, I looked around the operating room, in total disbelief of what was really happening. Tears began to fall from my eyes. The nurse saw my tears and wiped my eyes with her hands.

"Everything will be okay sweetheart," she said. "It will all get better in time."

CRYSTAL RAY

Before I knew it, the anesthesia had kicked in and I was out. I woke up from surgery and my friend was sitting right beside me. She then took me to the store to get a few things and I went home and slept and cried. After the surgery, I was outraged. I was mad at Derrick. He didn't show up at all. He called me the next day and apologized, saying he had a meeting with his family. I told him that it was best for us to part ways, breaking my heart all the more. I began to think of all the negative things he said, plus how I was treated at church. I had gone back to church, only to hear his dad say from the pulpit that he didn't want any grandkids outside of wedlock and then he shared his desire of having lots of grandsons but that they must be born in wedlock. I left and cried in the car. I blamed God for killing my baby to please the man of God. At that moment, I was sure that God loved them more and cared about their desires more.

Some time later, I returned to the church. Six months had passed and I was finally getting back to normal. I decided that a vacation was the perfect way to start over. It was my first vacation, I went to visit one of my best friends in San Diego. This was my first time getting on an airplane, first visit to California, and my first time ever seeing the ocean. I had fun and I processed a lot. I thought about my life, my children because I had never traveled without them, and I thought about Derrick. I wondered if he thought about me. I wondered if he still cared about me or if he was relieved. There were so many unanswered questions because the relationship ended without closure. I came to grips that I did miss him but he didn't protect me like he said he would. He wasn't there for me.

A month after my vacation, guess who reaches out to me on Facebook? Derrick. He inboxed me that he hoped I was doing well, that he really missed me, and that he had a lot of time to think and he was so sorry for all the hurt he caused. He then asked if we could talk because he'd rather tell me in person. I got my number changed after the incident. I knew that was the only way I was going to be able to move forward, especially now that he lived in another state. I could tell that he was sincere, so I told him I'd give him a call. I intentionally waited a few days before texting him. He was not getting easy access to me. Finally, he called and apologized. He said he was so excited to hear my voice. I was kind of excited to hear his, too.

We talked about all that happened and ended the conversation on a good note. He then started trying to work his way back into my heart. It was not easy, but he persisted. Though we were distant, we had a love that would travel distances just to give each other a hug and to be in each other's presence. He had a love for me that helped heal some of my inner hurts. He asked me if I was willing to meet him because he really wanted to see me. I agreed to visit and we agreed to meet up in Joplin, MO. It was a hot drive. Summer was blazing. When he saw me get out of the car, he lit just as he always did. He told me I was beautiful in my bright summer dress. He then went to his car and pulled out an enormous brown teddy bear and gave it to me.

"I remember you told me you had bear when you were younger that got destroyed and how much you loved that bear," he said. "I saw this and thought of you. Since I'm gone you can hold him and think of me."

Mr. Bear was nowhere near the size of that bear. He wasn't a miniature teddy bear, but he was miniature in comparison to that bear. That bear was almost as tall as me. The bear was very thoughtful. We ate and talked for hours, totally losing track of time. I was too tired to travel, plus I was afraid to drive back alone in the dark. We found a hotel for me to stay in, but he had to leave. He could tell I was afraid to stay in a strange town by myself. He said that he would leave after he knew I was asleep.

We watched tv but he ended up falling asleep, too. I woke up to him staring at me.

"I miss you so much and I still love you," he said.

I looked in his eyes and I told him, "Ditto."

I felt a sense of relief from his heart, its like he needed to hear that. He pulled me closer and kissed me. There was so much passion, remorse, and joy in that kiss. I felt it, the ice heart that I had towards him was now melted. We had the best night until the next day when he started bugging me about taking the morning after pill. I agreed to take the pill, not even I wanted to experience the hell of that again. Especially since his family was talking to him again and he was about to move back home. I could see that he was happy again and so was I. I didn't want a baby to mess that up, so I took the pill. The pill made my cycle start early. It totally threw my body way off. A few weeks later, I found out that was pregnant. After accusing me of not taking the pill and me yelling at him because I did take it, Derrick calmed down and said it must be meant to be. He said that we would get through it. I was shocked. I thought he would go ballistic. His reaction scared me. He was calm and I wasn't.

Derrick was there for me in the beginning and then he started acting like a jerk. I wasn't a fan of his jerk side and to this day, I'm still not. It was almost as if he got pleasure from making me upset. I told him to leave me alone and that he needed to get it together. I guess the reality of the baby started to kick in because I started to show. I'm not sure if he was in denial at first, but my belly showing cleared that up. I knew he was afraid of others knowing, especially his family. I was concerned, too, because everyone could see that I was pregnant. I couldn't hide it anymore. I stopped going to church again. He finally told his family that I was pregnant when I was 7 or 8 months. The funny thing is that Derrick told me a few days before he told them that his mom had a dream that he had a son and that she played with the baby. She talked about how they needed to hurry and get him married so that the dream could become a reality.

"Well, thank you Lord for giving them a heads up that he was going to have a son," I thought. It just didn't happen according to their plans. The baby was only a few weeks away from being born. Of course, they were once again very upset, only this time, he wasn't banished and because the secret was out now, I came out of hiding and went back to church. Honestly, I had never been treated so horribly in my life. I was gossiped about, lied on, you name it. Rumor spread that I was just after the family's money because I was struggling as a single mom. I wasn't at all. Then there were rumors that the baby wasn't even his.

Closer to my due date, I decided that the stress was not good for me or the baby. I felt that it was in my best interest to no longer attend my church. I was on the verge of another boiling point and it was not going to be pretty had I continued. I was going to spill everything, to set the record straight and defend myself to leadership, folks that wanted to be in leadership, gossipers, sneaky freaks, and everybody else that needed to mind their freaking business. The Lord reminded me that was not a good choice, he reminded me of the woman I had become and not the women I was. He assured me that in His time and in His way, I would be vindicated and to pursue peace. Not long after, I gave birth to a healthy, beautiful, almost 10lb baby boy. It was something special about this kid. He was so loving and peaceful. Sadly, the other side of his family had a hard time accepting the situation. I wrote his family a letter, apologizing for any pain or shame I may have caused and that I really loved their son deeply. They never responded or even acknowledged my letter. I called child support and had paperwork sent to me so that a paternity test could be done. Even after the results proved that he was Derrick's son, they still had a hard time accepting the situation. Derrick, being torn by his love for me and the assurance of his family, became distant as well. He always shared with me that this was not easy for him and that he wished he could please everybody.

My authenticity was being tested greatly. This situation was getting harder by the days. To add insult to injury, when our son was almost a month old my friend called me to tell me that Derrick had gotten another woman pregnant and that I needed to move on with my life. I snapped on him. He brought out the old me. I seriously could have chopped his penis off. At that moment, I was done. I endured a lot from him, the church, his family, and his new baby momma. I got treated horribly while I was pregnant, but after the baby was born it got worse. I was so hurt by my church. I cried trying to figure out how people could preach love and mercy and not live it out. Not long afterwards, I was told that his new girlfriend had a miscarriage. She wasn't treated well either. I remember seeing her crying at a women's event. I walked over and gave her a hug and told her that she would get through this. She apologized for being so mean to me and asked me how I kept smiling and being strong.

She shared that she struggled deeply with the opinions of man. The church talked about her, too. She told me that I was such a strong woman and that I was so much stronger than she was. I held her and let her cry it out. That was major for me because that girl was very nasty towards me. However, I could tell she was struggling. It was written all over her face. I knew what she was going through. I walked it out twice and now even harder because of the baby. Although many were nasty towards me, God always sends a faithful few. Many would tell me that they always saw me as a great person. They knew I loved him, they knew he loved me, and how they would keep praying. Right now, things are slowly but surely progressing. There was small progress and I learned to be grateful for it. I prayed for years that God would turn this around and bring a blessing out of such a huge mess. I've taught myself not to hope for much, because it hurts too much. I stopped trying and lost faith that it would ever get better. I chose to let them do them and I will do me.

Honestly, this situation affected my life the most. None of the other traumas I faced hurt me and affected my life such as this one. Things got so bad that I suffered from major depression and suicidal thoughts. I even started having panic attacks. The major emotion that I dealt with during this was disappointment. This affected every area of my life, but mostly my faith in God and especially in church leadership. I thought that I finally had a life worth living, I didn't care about their wealth, that's why I never asked for a dime. I didn't care about getting their last name. Their son could've denied his name or even changed it to something else and it wouldn't have made me love him any more or less. I loved that man and I knew he loved me. He was just too immature at the time to take a stand.

I remember one day going to IHOP (International House of Prayer). This Asian lady came up to me to pray for me. I had been attending church online as a Potter's House e-member, so this was my first time going. This lady stood in front of me and prayed that I would see myself as the woman that God called me to be. She told me that she saw me ministering to thousands around the world. That I would travel and do great things for God and that I had a very big purpose on the earth.

"You've been hurt by church leadership and that the hurt was so deep that it was embedded in your subconscious mind," she said.

I thought I was over it, but it was still affecting me deeply. At this point, I'm balling my eyes out and my knees were weak.

She also said, "The Lord wants you to know that He loves you so much and that He's always loved you and how they treated you was not a reflection of His heart towards you."

After hearing this, I was on the floor in tears. She continued to build me up in the faith and promised me that God had great plans me for me. I did not go through all of that because I was a nobody. I endured that because I was someone great and that God would get the glory out of this situation. Talk about being wrecked in the Spirit! I needed that like I needed air to breathe. I needed to know His heart towards me. I needed to know that I wasn't going crazy.

Many years have passed since this and I am still healing. Two years ago, I was finally able to dare to love again. I hoped and prayed for years that God would fix the situation for all of us and make it good. I thought that I was completely over my son's father and trained myself to be numb towards him because I couldn't handle the thought of loving him. It hurts to not be able to freely express the desires of your heart. To this day, I have never loved a man the way that I loved him. Sometimes, I wonder if I ever will. I believe I will. It was hard to rebuild after crushed dreams and a broken heart but I am more and more each day. I finally got to a place in which if they never apologize or acknowledged my hurts that I would still walk in love and strive to be the best I can be. I truly know in my heart that they are good people that have experienced hurt and pain as well. They responded out of their own experiences.

Over the years I have learned how to put this behind me and to see them in a positive light. I'm truly grateful for them. They were my secret agents of change. God used them to reveal my true identity in Him and this situation revealed my God to me. I may not have been what they wanted for their family but God has always wanted me. He knew who I was but also who I would become, regardless of whether they or I saw it. Because of this, I grew an intimate relationship with Him. It was more than going to church, more than volunteering. I know HIM now. He brought me out again, He stayed with me, and because of this my heart smiles.

I've grown and learned so much over the years. The disappointment that once plagued my heart for years, I now have a new perspective. I now see my troubles as areas to grow in my faith and teach me how to pray. I rejoice freely because I have an even greater relationship with my Creator and Father! This relationship was meant to last forever! Because He is a God of wonders, I know that in the right time and in the right way He will turn this around as well, just as He's done before.

Disappointed Heart

Again, no not again!

Whats the point of this, why did I have to endure?

A heart full of pain and sorrow, a heart so pure.

I hoped and I prayed for the best of things to come.

Yet I was left with grief, with lost, my heart is now numb.

Whats the meaning of this, whats the plan?

Im lost and confused, when will it end.

My purpose seems silent, and answer yet ignore.

The groans of my heart that is bleeding on the floor.

One day Ill be free, Ill love, Ill understand again.

That blessed day my disappointment will end.

Chapter 7: It's Not Always as it Appears

Now enough about my mess. If you're anything like me, you too have encountered multiple traumatic experiences. Trust me, the ones I've talked about are only a few. For years, I wondered what was wrong with me. Why do I keep getting into these types of situations? Did I do something to deserve all the pain I've experienced? The question of my life thus far has been, when will things turn around for me? When will I experience happiness, better yet, joy? I've endured so many sorrows. Does joy even exist? I never understood why it seems as if joy embraces some while rejecting others. How does a very loving and giving person's life be reduced to suffering? Thinking back on my life there were times of laughter, but the times I've cried outnumbered the times I've smiled. What I've come to know and I am still learning, is that joy doesn't come when things are going well. I didn't find joy in asking questions and pondering upon the pain. I found joy when I shifted my focus off my pain and I looked at all that was left intact.

Although I've been through a lot, I'm still here. You see, I spent most of my life waiting on life to send me better days, not even realizing that I had the choice and the power to stop waiting for them and create them. I'm not making light of what I've experienced or what you may have experienced. I only chose to make a conscious decision to no longer allow anger, fear, shame, confusion, and disappointment to dictate my life. We cannot change our past, but what we can do is choose to live a damn good future. The moment I stopped embracing my pain and I started embracing the possibility of better days contrary to my current circumstances - this was my joy factor!

Yes, it hurt. Yes, it cost me greatly, but I made it through! I survived it all! I may be broken but I'm now being mended. Although the wicked things of life tried to destroy me, yet I live. The beauty of this is that I get to share my story with you. My pain has created numerous opportunities and I've met so many wonderful people in the process. I've met broken people just like me. I've even met those that are more broken than I am and those that are yet hiding in denial. I sit here before you today, unashamed and letting you know that nothing in my current life has shifted yet. I'm now living with my dad. I lost my home, car, and everything. Nothing that I hoped for has happened yet. However, just because it hasn't happened yet, does not mean it's not on the way. Think of a pregnancy; the baby is developing on the inside, the mother cannot see or feel the baby for a while. Just because she cannot see it, doesn't mean that things aren't happening. She will give birth in due time. So will I and so will you.

A mind that thinks it's going nowhere always arrives at its desired destination. A mind that knows it's going somewhere will always arrive at its destination as well. Because of life's experiences and how people treated me, I thought I was a nobody and I did what nobodies do. Then I came to this revelation because of the depth of my pain; I was not only somebody, but a big somebody! The bigger your trouble, the bigger your purpose is! Grab ahold of that and hold it tight!

The things in my life that I thought I needed and the people who I thought I couldn't live without, I now realize that I have outgrown them both. I don't need either to enjoy my life. The greatest thing I've needed was not people or things, but a new mindset. I desperately needed a fresh outlook on myself and my situations. I gave myself permission to not view my life from the rearview mirror, but to look forward to the endless possibilities that await. I didn't start with confronting my past even though I had to face it. I started with embracing me and getting to know myself without the opinions and pressures of others and how they see me. In getting to know myself, I saw that what lies beneath was a beautiful soul and beautiful woman.

I allowed myself to try new things, meet new people, and go new places. Guess what, I did it intentionally. We are not always going to feel like it or want to explore new things. I dare you to press past all the reasons you shouldn't step into the new and do it anyway. If things don't go according to your expectations, you're not losing, you're learning.

I learned something interesting about myself and it makes absolutely no sense at all, but it's okay. I've prided myself in the joy of isolation. It was my safety net. Then I started hanging out with people and I loved it when I wanted to be bothered but I hated it when I didn't. It didn't matter how much I love or like a person, when I want to be alone, I want to be alone. I know it's crazy, but it's me. In my dealings with others, I've grown to love and desire the power of connection. I didn't realize how afraid I was of connecting with other people. Amid the fear, I was even more determined to not allow it to put me back into my safety bubble. I then made a conscious decision to love the people around me anyway, knowing that they may hurt me but just like everything else in my life, this too shall pass.

I also found joy when I stopped focusing on what I wanted and I started focusing on and appreciating what I had. I began to build a new life upon what I have and where I am today. Being mindful of what I can do, not what I can't; who I have now, not those that have left. People, circumstances, and stuff will always change, heck even I've changed. My old Pastor David Blunt always said, "When something isn't growing, its dying." This death is a slow death starting within and manifesting itself outwardly.

I got tired of dying and chose the uncomfortable journey of growth. Through the changes of life there has only been one constant in my life. One thing remained the same. Regardless of my heart, attitude, situations, and behaviors, my God was there. Many people give honor to that which has helped them overcome and they have a freedom and a choice to do so. As for me, my faith in God and who He is, is the very reason I'm still here. After reading my story, you may think you can't trust my God. He let me experience so many horrible things. Although that may be a fact, it's not the whole truth. The way my life appears isn't what it is at all. Yes, He decided not to rescue me from every evil thing that came my way. The beauty of this is because He was with me, I overcame everything that was against me.

There were times when I sought to see His hand and I saw just that. Meanwhile there were other times I sought after His hand and I didn't see it. Because I didn't see His hand I thought he abandoned me, too. Evidence of His hands meant that I was out of it. The moments when the lesson was not to get me out, I had to learn to see His footprints. His footprints revealed to me that He was with me, even when it was hard and when I wanted to give up. I felt so alone at times but when I remembered that He was with me, I was comforted. My whole life I wished, hoped, and prayed that someone would be there and just love me through. I can't count how many times I've desired to feel special, to feel as though I mattered to at least one person. I looked for validation in people and in situations. The lack of their validation made me feel ugly, unloved, and unwanted. I was so lost and wrapped up in the opinions of people and the dependency of their love to make me feel valuable. A love with great frailties, a love that only loved me when I did what it wanted.

Because of this, I did and said some crazy and stupid things to obtain the love and affection of others. I saw that this was getting me nowhere. So I stopped looking at the people in my life that attempted to love me but failed and I set them free from their attempts, no longer judging them.

Instantly, I was met with a new heart and a new awareness. I now saw that I was so blinded in my mess that I failed to see the hand and footprints of love were always there. When I acknowledged and embraced this love, I was loved back to health and soundness of mind. I began to see myself as loved and greatly loved. I saw my purpose and it was great, too. Nothing in my life was ever going to change that. Nothing I have faced or will face will ever change His love and plan for me.

We often think of love as an expression of happiness and never experience anything contrary to that. Some will deny the nature and existence of His love for me because I've experienced unpleasant times. Marriages and relationships experience unpleasant times all the time and yet it does not detract the love they share. So it is with my God. My pains revealed Him to me. He allowed it to be so that I could know Him. In knowing Him,

CRYSTAL RAY

I know the power and the authority that He has given me to overcome anything in Him. What I know of Him is this; He is good, and all good things come from Him.

What I find the most interesting is that God is often blamed when evil things occur as if He did it himself. Thoughts such as these only exist when we don't know and fully understand Him and His ways. We know that evil exists, we see it every day. Now if God is good and the source of all things good, how can He be evil and do evil? I had to learn that we live in an evil world brought upon by the powers of darkness. Darkness has a purpose, just as light does. Many of us, because of our dark days, know light and appreciate it even more. I had to learn to see God as He is and not how He is portrayed.

As I matured in the knowledge and wisdom of Him, I stopped blaming Him as the source of my pain. Yes, He had the power and the ability to give me new life, but what I didn't see or understand was that He had given me the same power and ability to change it myself. He wanted me to exercise what He had given me. I didn't know that everything I accused God of not doing, He had already equipped me to do it with Him. When I got the revelation that God needed me on board with what He wanted to do in the earth and in my life, it all made great sense. Every evil thing I've faced was caused by a person, including myself. Evil needs a person to operate through. The evil things that I endured in life were not from God, they were from people who allowed themselves to be a vessel used for evil.

God's plan for your mess is to turn that mess into something beautiful, if you will let Him. I cannot force you, He will not force you either. He has given you the right to decide for yourself. It's a choice we must all make. I had to be willing to drink from the fullness of His love and who He created me to be and be satisfied, completely satisfied. This mess of a life I have experienced is now filled with so much inward beauty and joy.

My greatest desire is for you to dare to know and embrace the beauty of your story because of who is with you and who is sustaining you. He loves you and wants to give you beauty in the midst of your mess. How do I know He loves you? How do I know He wants to give you beauty? Because He sent me to you to share our love so that He could reach you. He saw me through all that I've experienced, knowing that you would one day be faced with your own troubles. He knew that you would come across this book that will ignite something in you.

He also said in His Word, in one of the most life-giving scriptures to me, *"The Spirit of the LORD is on me, because the LORD has anointed me to proclaim good news to the poor. He has sent me to bind up the brokenhearted, to proclaim freedom for the captives and release from darkness for the prisoners, to proclaim the year of the LORDs favor and the day of vengeance of our God, to comfort all who mourn, and provide those who grieve, to bestow on them a crown of beauty instead of ashes, the oil of joy instead of mourning, and a garment of praise instead of a spirit of despair,"* Isaiah 61:1-3.

I dare you to see yourself differently, not by your mistakes, pains, and disappointments. The same person that was with me is with you now; waiting on your acknowledgment, waiting to turn your pain into joy. I stand here today, no longer overwhelmed or depressed by the things that happened to me but rather joyous in the woman that I've become because of them. Even the desires of my heart that I eagerly wait for, do not hinder my joy. It doesn't have to begin when they arrive because I choose to smile now. The power that lies within me allows me to define what joy is to me. I choose to rest in the beauty of all that is taking place within me.

This beautiful mess that I call myself is a rose that once tried to survive in desert-like conditions. It was wilting and dying by the sources that once fed me, the shame, anger, fear, disappointment, and confusion that plague my life so. Although it appears that I am still living in lacking, I know I have underground springs sustaining me. My greatest transformation was changing my perspective on how I saw myself and the life I lived. Since then I've been replanted in the beauty of my new mind and God's love. My Creator is the source of my beauty. I am a rose on display for all to see.

O BEAUTIFUL MESS

Great beauty lies in your mess as well. I dare you to see it. Don't let what happened to you or what didn't go right in the past rob you of a glorious future. Set your own standards and compare yourself to no one. You're one of a kind. The opinions of man are just that; opinions! Allow yourself to love again and receive love in return. With all your hurts and pains and ups and downs, celebrate the beauty of you! Let the light of your life shine bright and don't forget to help someone else find the light that is buried inside of them as well.

Bless the day that joy came in.

The beauty of love, a new day begins.

The joy of His love has kept my heart.

Oh I wish I knew of this love from the start.

My heart all aglow now, such radiance, such light

The colors of joy so warm and so bright.

I've learned to free those that once hurt me

A heart now healed, so alive and free

My heart sings a new song and its lovely too.

Because I'm free from the old, I now live in the new!

Chapter 8: The Greatest Gift

I would like to extend to you what was extended to me. I told you who made my life brand new and who turned my mess into not only something beautiful, but someone beautiful. I do not look like all that I've been through, inwardly or outwardly. I take no credit for overcoming the things I went through. Please know that I'm not forcing or imposing my beliefs on you. It is totally your choice. I cannot speak for what may work for others, I can only say what worked and is still working in my life and that is a relationship with Jesus. He made the difference in my life and He turned it all around for my good, just as He said He would. To receive the freedom that I received, you have to accept Him, acknowledge His saving grace, and ask Him for help. Trusting and believing that He alone, the Creator of life, gives new life. The Bible states that "whosoever, shall call on the name of the Lord shall be saved."

This not only is the start of a new earthly life, but it's your ticket into an even greater eternal life to come. If you are ready, confess with your mouth and believe in your heart that Jesus paid the ultimate price unto death to give you new life in Him. Ask Him to forgive your sins and to help you live a better life. I couldn't do it without Him. If I had the option to do it all over again, my heart will declare that better is one day with Him than thousands without Him. You have a love that is willing to help you and cover you, all your wrongs, hurts, and whatever you may be dealing with. All you have to do is ask.

Now that you have asked Him for forgiveness, do yourself a favor. Bless yourself with the greatest gift of forgiving yourself and all those who hurt you. To be forgiven of our sins, we must forgive others of theirs. What do you really have to lose? If I'm wrong about Jesus, you technically have nothing to lose, but if I am right about Him and you've rejected His invitation, you will lose it all, especially in the life to come. Your access will be denied because you showed up to board a new life with the wrong boarding pass. I don't want that to happen to you. If this book has changed your life for the good and if you are now my brother or sister in Christ, I want to hear from you! I would love to hear your story!

About the Author

Photo credit: Shalese Johnson

Crystal Ray is a writer, motivational speaker, and teacher. A loving mother of three boys, Matthew, Samuel, and Jayden. She loves to spend her days living the simple life of faith, family, friends and fun. Crystal Ray has a passion and vision to touch the hearts of the hurting. To uplift and build those who society counts as insignificant. To let the light of love outshine the darkness we face daily.

Made in the USA
Lexington, KY
22 July 2019